A World of Faith

Carolyn Pogue

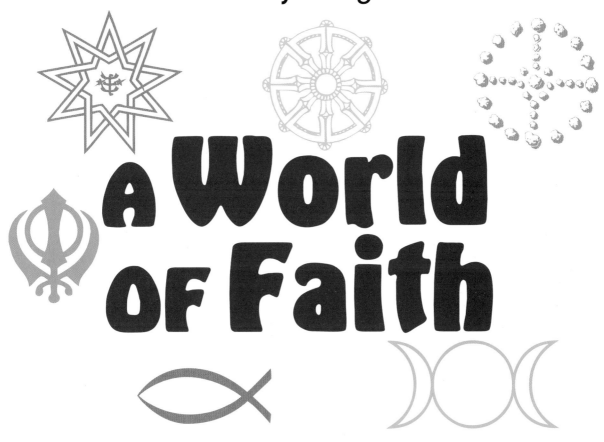

A World of Faith

Introducing Spiritual Traditions to Teens

CopperHouse

Editors: Monica Plant and Mike Schwarzentruber
Cover design: Margaret Kyle and Verena Velten
Interior design: Verena Velten
Proofreader: Heather Picotte
See page 191 for photo/illustration credits

CopperHouse is an imprint of Wood Lake Publishing, Inc. Wood Lake Publishing acknowledges the financial support of the Government of Canada, through the Book Publishing Industry Development Program (BPIDP) for its publishing activities. Wood Lake Publishing also acknowledges the financial support of the Province of British Columbia through the Book Publishing Tax Credit.

At Wood Lake Publishing, we practise what we publish, being guided by a concern for fairness, justice, and equal opportunity in all of our relationships with employees and customers. Wood Lake Publishing is an employee-owned company, committed to caring for the environment and all creation. Wood Lake Publishing recycles, reuses, and encourages readers to do the same. Resources are printed on 100% post-consumer recycled paper and more environmentally friendly groundwood papers (newsprint), whenever possible. A percentage of all profit is donated to charitable organizations.

Library and Archives Canada Cataloguing in Publication
Pogue, Carolyn, 1948-
A world of faith: introducing spiritual traditions to teens / Carolyn Pogue.
Includes bibliographical references and index.
ISBN 978-1-55145-554-9
1. Religions. 2. Teenagers–Religious life. I. Title.
BL80.3.P63 2007   200.835   C2007-904344-5

Published by CopperHouse
An imprint of Wood Lake Publishing Inc.
9590 Jim Bailey Road, Kelowna, BC, Canada, V4V 1R2
www.woodlakebooks.com
250.766.2778

Printing 10 9 8 7 6 5 4 3 2 1
Printed in Canada by Transcontinental

Dedication

This book is dedicated to

Nina, Forest, Shoshana, Ryan, Nguyen,
Arvind, Maren, Ramya, Farah,
and to all young people working for a better world.

Table of Contents

Acknowledgements

Thank you to the people from the various faith traditions who read chapters in a range of states of completion: Dr. Ronnie Joy Leah, Fiona MacGregor, Jeannette Sinclair, Myra Laramee, Dr. Gita Das, Rabbi Howard voss Altman, Lynn Chazotsang, Very Reverend Bill Phipps, Ryan J. White, Dr. Harjot Kaur Singh, Kathy Madiji, Dr. Zohra Husaini, and Reverend Clint Mooney.

Thank you for research, connections, and encouragement to Doreen Masran; Margaret Theophile; Diane D'Souza; Karen Hamdon; Doreen Orman; Deborah Moldow of the World Peace Prayer Society; Yashio Mochizuki of The Goi Peace Foundation; Raffi Cavoukian, founder of Child Honouring; to Abby Willowroot for her prayer in Chapter 1; and to the Sinclair family for permission to quote from Lorraine's work.

I value the support and insights of the multi-faith group Women in Spirituality in Calgary.

I thank the Faith and the Common Good network for permission to use their collection of "Green Rules," and Scarboro Missions for permission to use their collection of "Golden Rules," which you will see at the beginning and end of each chapter. I had a lot of help with this book, but the omissions and errors belong to me.

Thank you to the teens who shared their wisdom: Forest Whitlow, Ramya Gopal, Nina Ha, Shoshana Wolf, Ryan Workman, Arvind Bhatia, Farah Hattab, and Maren Stachnik. This book is for you.

Thank you to peacemakers of every faith tradition around the planet who bravely walk the path of healing and often swim against the current.

As ever and always, thank you to beloved Bill, who walks with me and shares his vision for a peaceful world.

Foreword by HRH Prince El Hassan bin Talal

Our faiths command us not to sit idly by amid mounting hostility and mistrust, but to make a substantial contribution to peace-building in a polarized world. We must avoid the polarities of truth that have come to drive the international agenda. We can promote a middle way that is not only ethically right, but strategically prudent. *One way to begin is by learning about one another's spiritual traditions.*

Our role *as people of faith* is to be an ever-present reminder to political leaders that it is an ethic of human solidarity that has ensured humanity's survival and well-being from time immemorial. That ethic is based on shared values such as respect, responsibility, and selflessness.

Reconciliation stands little chance when narrow-minded extremists are bloodletting and sowing division in the name of our respective faiths. Our essential religious values are utterly incompatible with the cycles of retribution making the headlines today.

Shared values lead to shared security. The vast majority of people belong to religious communities. We *can help to address extremism* by exploring common values and by refusing to let political divides be elevated to religious status.

The world's major religions share the essential belief that compassion is the key to spiritual awareness, and that compassion does not mean just detached sympathy for others but active engagement with them. Belief means action, and we must act.

All our ancient faiths and philosophies remain profoundly relevant in this troubled time. Our faiths remind us that it is vital to recognise the humanity of the other in order to affirm our own humanity. In that sense, interfaith dialogue must be linked practically and meaningfully with political dialogue. It must be a parallel process rather than a pleasant afterthought. This is how we can restore the peaceful role of our faiths when it is needed most.

Understanding one another's spiritual traditions is a step toward achieving a more peaceful world. A good companion on that journey is A World of Faith: Introducing Spiritual Traditions to Teens. *This unique book breaks new ground in interpreting the world's religions and will be an inspiration to creating a Culture of Peace.* Attending the Religions for Peace Youth Assembly in Kyoto last year assured me that a creative hope thrives in the next generation.

In peace,

HRH Prince El Hassan bin Talal

The President Emeritus of *Religions for Peace*, 2007

Introduction

A friendly study of all the scriptures is the sacred duty of every individual.

~ GANDHI

Humans everywhere have always been connected by wind, water, and soil. The water I drink may once have flowed down the Ganges River or been part of an iceberg near Newfoundland. Throughout history, humans have also been connected by something invisible – a common, deep-rooted awareness that we are spiritual beings.

We know instinctively that there is more to life than what we can see, touch, measure, control, or package. Sometimes we recognize it when we come face to face with it, other times we miss it completely. Sometimes we have words to express what we are feeling, other times we are left speechless. In this way, I think spirituality is like love. We can experience it, but we

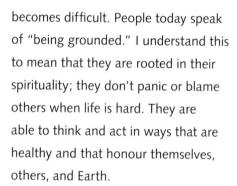

don't always have words to describe it. To figure it out, we might need to sit with a friend and sort through our feelings and thoughts, compare experiences, or talk about books or movies that have helped shape our ideas about what love actually is. Just as great and beautiful things grow out of love, great and beautiful things can grow out of spirituality.

I also think spirituality is like soil. This is where our roots are. This is what nourishes our souls and anchors us so that we don't blow away when life becomes difficult. People today speak of "being grounded." I understand this to mean that they are rooted in their spirituality; they don't panic or blame others when life is hard. They are able to think and act in ways that are healthy and that honour themselves, others, and Earth.

Out of this spirituality, our ancestors developed rituals, beliefs and ceremonies, and passed them on from one generation to the next. Some spiritual traditions have continued since the beginning of time and are rooted in the land, such as Aboriginal spirituality.

Other traditions, such as Judaism, became part of a religion centred on the teachings and life stories of particular people. Culture and geography shape how traditions have been formed and are practised. Today the people of a variety of faith traditions are learning from each other.

The three faiths that came from Abraham – Judaism, Christianity, and Islam – all have Ten Commandments in their sacred writings. Children learn them at an early age. One commandment says, "Honour your father and mother." It's a good commandment that directs us to look back in history. In Haudenosaunee (Iroquois) sacred teachings, we learn that we should honour our Elders, and we should also honour the seventh generation. This means that when making political, economic, or other decisions, leaders must consider the impact on their great, great, great, great, great, great-grandchildren. Non-native people are learning from this philosophy and see how decisions with short-term vision have hurt the planet.

In this book you will see how our ancestors had a spiritual concept of

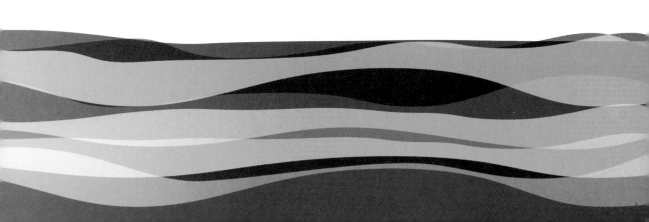

the Goddess. You will catch glimpses of how this concept connects to many traditions developed later. This book moves in chronological order from the Goddess tradition through to the Bahá'í faith – from the oldest to most recent. There is also a chapter called "Multifaith World: Only One Planet," which explores how organizations help bring together the human family on our fragile planet. The appendices have information about traditions not covered in this book, information about cults, words from daughter and mother peacemakers, and suggestions for other sources of information.

I hope that you'll discover answers to questions you might have, and some questions to answers you have too. I hope that you enjoy the freedom you have to practise the spiritual tradition of your choice, knowing that in some parts of the world people die for this right.

The world needs people who care about our global neighbourhood. Eminent scientist David Suzuki says, "We invent our future every day. Choose wisely." Every day creative and wonderful ideas are tried that bring people together to learn, explore common ground, and find ways to create a culture of peace. My prayer is that this book can be a small tool for building a world fit for teens and other living beings on this good green Earth.

In the name of all that we say is holy, how can we help each other to make Earth clean and safe for the seventh generation? What sacred stories of hope can you tell me? What stories of courage can I share with you? Let's have a meal together and make some plans. Let's not waste time.

May peace prevail.

Chapter 1

Goddess Tradition

Green Rule

Do unto Earth
as you would have
Earth do unto you.

A Prayer for Strength

Goddess Mother help me

to be patient and strong

to see what is truly important

to act without selfishness or fear

Goddess Mother help me

to trust your wisdom

to resist the coward's way

to walk in faith and compassion

to be truly human in spirit and heart

~ Abby Willowroot, 2000. Used by permission.
www.spiralgoddess.com/Homage.html

Tradition

Imagine living in peace and harmony. Many believe that societies did just that when the Goddess culture was predominant. Because some archaeologists have not found fortified buildings or walls around these communities, they believe that the people back then valued and lived in peace. Goddess statues have been found in many parts of the world and some date back 30,000 years. Archeologists believe that in these communities, men and women enjoyed equal status and that families were matrilineal (based on the female line). Eventually, and

Thumbnail Sketch

Who was the founder?
There was no one founder. The Goddess tradition evolved around the world as people understood their dependence on Earth and the power of it.

When did it start? In the beginning, tens of thousands of years ago.

Were there any foundational sacred texts?
Rather than books, all of life was viewed as sacred, including earth, water, air, fire, animals, and phases of the moon.

The Triple Goddess Concept

Three phases of the moon (waxing, full, waning) symbolize the three aspects of the Triple Goddess. The waxing or new moon symbolizes childhood, the full moon symbolizes adulthood and the waning or crescent moon symbolizes old age. Put together, the symbols of these three phases make up a single symbol: a circle with two mirrored crescents on either side.

The fourth phase of the moon is also important to know about: it is the dark moon, the three days at the end of each lunar cycle when we cannot see the moon. The dark moon symbolizes death, the pause before rebirth. The four phases of the moon and what they symbolize can also be aligned with seasons – spring, summer, fall and winter.

over centuries, another version of reality surfaced. People who believed in war, male gods, and the suppression of nature, mixed in with and finally gained power over the Goddess societies. Equality between men and women became a thing of the past, and women's power was dismissed or women oppressed. Menstruation, once viewed as sacred, took on other names such as "the curse" and women became viewed as unclean. The wisdom of old women, once valued, became dismissed as "old wives' tales."

As organized religions gained strength, Goddess, priestess and mother were replaced by God, priest and father. Patriarchy restricted women's political, religious, and even domestic power. In some religious writings we read that women were viewed as possessions of their fathers, husbands or other male relatives. Goddess worship became a sin. Violence against women became acceptable. In Europe especially, but in other places as well, women suffered particularly, along with

In what places did people worship? Everywhere and anywhere.

What were worship leaders called? Shamans, priests, or priestesses.

Where was the tradition practised? Worldwide.

Were there special holy days? Summer and winter solstices, spring and fall equinoxes, full moon and new moon. The calendar was lunar, which means that the dates of the holy days changed according to the cycles of the moon.

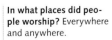

The Egg and Creation Stories

From ancient times the egg has been a symbol of life and a symbol of mystery. Although an egg appears dead, it holds the mystery and wonder of new life. There are many stories about the cosmic egg told in far-flung places such as Australia, Tibet and countries in Africa.

The ancient Greeks told a story about the Goddess of All Things emerging from Chaos. In the beginning, they say Eurynome (whose name means "wide-wandering") was very lonely. She magically took the form of a dove and laid an amazing egg, the Universal Egg. She asked a serpent to coil around it seven times and care for the egg until it was ready to crack open.

When it hatched, the earth tumbled out, the sun and moon, the flowers, humans and all of creation. This was the beginning of the world.

In India, an ancient creation story

the Roman church went on a rampage during the decades-long Inquisition.

Although there is disagreement among archaeologists about some aspects of this spirituality, the tradition of the Goddess left clues to its structure, focus, rituals and beliefs. One clue is the amazing art that has been left inside caves, in graves and on the walls of cliffs and dwellings in many different parts of the world. This art includes paintings and beautiful sculptures showing clearly that the feminine form was valued, that the miracles of childbirth and breastfeeding were held in awe, and that the seasons of a woman's life and the seasons of planting and harvesting were linked. The cycles of the moon and the concept of rebirth were also shown in art. One of the oldest statues of the Goddess dates back about 30,000 years. Named the Venus of Willendorf (the statue was found near Willendorf, Austria), this simple statue is of an ample woman's body, her hands resting on her breasts in a nurturing pose. Her hair is arranged like braids in rows, which perhaps symbolize the labyrinth.

Words to Know

Fall Equinox: the time when day and night are equal in length (around September 21).

Gaia: the Greek goddess of Earth. Gaia theory says that the whole Earth is one living organism and that people, animals, water – everything – are simply parts of it. Gaia could be considered the Great Goddess. There are other goddesses, too, like Sedna, the sea goddess; and Tara, goddess of peace and protection.

Neo-Pagan: nature-centred and pantheistic religion. (*Neo* means "new.")

Pagan: country-dweller; one who reveres nature.

Pantheism: the idea that the divine is in all creation.

Patriarchy: male-dominated leadership and control of a society.

tells that in the beginning, when there was only water, the waters decided to produce life. They did this by creating a golden egg that floated in the waves. After a year a human was hatched from the egg, and that is how life began.

Oestre or Eostar was a feast of the goddess Ishtar, who was also called Astarte or Esther. The egg was a symbol for Eostar because it represented the rebirth of the goddess and the bursting forth of nature. Since ancient times rabbits have been a symbol of sex and fertility. In Egypt, a rabbit, representing the god of resurrection (Osiris), was sacrificed to the Nile River each year as part of a prayer that the Nile would flood and fertilize the crops with rich river soil. The rabbit was also associated with goddesses in Europe, China, and ancient North America. Today it is little wonder that the images of the hare and egg continue to appear during springtime; they are universal symbols.

Another clue to Goddess beliefs can be found in stories. First told by parents to children around the fire under the wide night sky, then by lamplight or candlelight in mud, thatch, hide or stone houses, these stories were eventually written down and passed through generation after generation to our present time. The Greeks and Egyptians, for example, have left us a rich treasure of Goddess stories. When we learn these stories, we see that they pop up in a variety of places within religions, within folk tales passed down through the generations and in symbols that show up in various places in the world. One example is the symbol of the sacred tree, or tree of life, which appears in many traditions ranging from ancient Egypt to the beginnings of Judaism

Spring Equinox: the time when day and night are equal in length (around March 21). After the spring equinox, the sun follows a rising path through the sky, and days grow longer until the sun reaches its highest point on the summer solstice. During the fall equinox, the opposite occurs.

Summer Solstice: the longest day of the year (on or around June 21).

Wicca: goddess-worshipping, nature-centred mystery religion.

Winter Solstice: the shortest day of the year (on or around December 21). Many ancient structures, such as Stonehenge in England, capture sunlight or create shadows only during the equinox or solstice. Stories about the exact reason these structures were built have been lost.

The Tree

The tree is prevalent in many religions and spiritualities as a life-giving symbol; it was certainly important in the Goddess tradition. In some traditions the tree is seen as both a feminine symbol, providing nourishment like nuts and fruit and a home for birds, and as a male symbol, symbolizing the phallus. Its branches reach into the sky, its trunk is at human level and its roots reach down into the deepest, secret places of Earth so that the tree is seen to connect Earth, heaven and the underworld. In Mayan mythology, the sacred, heavenly Yaxche tree was where good people would go after death for protection and reward. An ancient Egyptian story tells of how Osiris was tricked, trapped in a coffin and thrown into the Nile River. The river deposited the coffin at the foot of the Tree of Life (a tamarisk), which grew up around the coffin and protected Osiris until he was rescued by Isis, the Mother Goddess.

and, afterwards, Christianity. Another example is the egg, which appears not only on our breakfast tables but as a decorated work of art or as a sweet brought by a mysterious rabbit at the time of the spring equinox.

Although the ancient worship of the Goddess was systematically attacked by patriarchy for centuries in most parts of the world, and by most religions, a quick Internet search or stroll through bookstores and libraries shows a great revival of interest and connection. When we consider today the importance of honouring Earth as the mother of all, we see that the Goddess beliefs make sense. Without a healthy planet, we will all become ill. Without a healthy planet, we will have no where else to go. We know, deep in our memories, that to honour, love and protect Earth is to honour, love and protect ourselves, our children and grandchildren. These days scientists like David Suzuki are telling us the same thing.

The Pentacle

The pentacle, a five-pointed star within a circle, is a widely recognized symbol of Wicca. It represents the integration of body and spirit, and also the four elements: fire, wind, water and earth. This symbol is sometimes viewed with suspicion and fear; it can even be dangerous to wear it. In May 2006, the Associated Press carried a story about an American war widow who wanted the pentacle on the grave of her husband, a soldier killed in Afghanistan. The Department of Veterans Affairs refused the family's request to have the symbol on his plaque.

The Goddess Today

Many traditional religions such as Judaism and Christianity, too, are looking back into their holy writings and reconsidering them from a feminist perspective while reclaiming their original connection with Earth. Some newer religions, such as Wicca, which began its revival in England in the 1940s, are gaining popularity in Europe and North America.

Eco-feminism surfaced as part of the women's movement when people began to make the connection between the body of Earth and women's bodies. People saw that both women's bodies and Earth were being used in unhealthy ways. War, greed, pollution and sexism all affect girls and women in particular ways as well as the health of the planet. In the 1970s, religious people began making the connection between a patriarchal understanding of religion and ecology. This awakening was energized by the

Sedna: A Goddess of the North

The story of Sedna, goddess of the sea, is an example of an ancient goddess who warns humans to care about their planet. Her story is told in the area around the North Pole among the people who live near the Arctic coasts.

When Sedna was young, many men wanted to marry her. She refused them all until one very persuasive man tempted her by promising a life of luxury. The newlyweds paddled a kayak to the man's

work of archaeologist Marija Gimbutas. Her study of neolithic cultures in Europe (from 6500 to 3500 BCE) revealed evidence of peaceful, woman-honouring and Goddess-worshipping societies where men and women were equal. Since the time of her work, there has been a better understanding that Earth is a sacred gift and that everyone must work to protect it. The Gaia theory, which sees the earth as a single organism, has helped people look in new ways at their old religious scriptures.

Around 1940, people in Britain began looking back at some of the ancient Goddess beliefs, such as those of the Celts and Druids. According to some scholars, this activity can also be traced back to the Romantic Movement in the

island home. When they arrived, Sedna learned an awful truth: he was not a kind human but a cruel birdman. Desperately she tried to escape but failed. One day her father visited. Together they killed the birdman and fled in his kayak.

But the birdman's friends avenged his death. They raised a terrible storm at sea. Sedna's father panicked and threw her overboard. Sedna clung to the side of the kayak, and wild with terror, her father chopped off her fingers one by one. Slowly, Sedna

sank to the sea bottom. As she sank, mysterious changes occurred. Sedna discovered she could breathe underwater. Her legs took the form of a fish tail. Her lost fingers transformed into whales, walruses, seals and fish. And Sedna became a

goddess with power over hunters and fishers of the sea. She could allow hunters and fishers to go home hungry or grant them luck with the hunt.

When food is scarce, a shaman visits Sedna in the dream world to comb her hair and

make her spirit happy. To this very day, they say Sedna warns people that, to avoid disaster, we must care for the sea and for all creatures living in the seas.

Rites of Passage

1800s as a reaction against the Industrial Revolution. Regardless of when they began, people had decided to revive some of the ancient ideas and to develop new ones. This revival resulted in a movement that is now also rooted in North America. The people who follow this practice are Wiccans. There are many books and Internet sites related to their practice. Both men and women practise Wicca. Their main concern is in honouring and healing Earth.

Menarche

When a girl began her first period (menarche or first menstruation), the women would gather to honour and welcome her into the second stage of life. In this stage, she stepped out of childhood and into a new place with the responsibilities and power of womanhood. This began her full-moon time. (See "Triple Goddess Concept" on p. 19.) The usual length of time between periods is the same as the cycle of the moon, 28 days. (The cycles of the moon taught people when to plant crops. It also measured the length of human pregnancies – ten lunar cycles.)

Rituals and Ceremonies

The rituals of Goddess worship revolved around the seasons of Earth, the cycles of the moon, and fertility.

Menopause

When a woman stopped menstruating, the women would gather to welcome her into the final phase of life. As a crone (old woman), wisdom and healing were most important. This began the waning-moon time. (See "Triple Goddess Concept" on p. 19.)

Golden Rule

Do whatever you will,

as long as it harms no one,

including yourself.

~ Wiccan Rede

Chapter 2

Aboriginal Spirituality

Green Rule

Only when the last tree has been cut down,
only after the last river has been poisoned,
only after the last fish has been caught, will
you find out that money cannot be eaten.

~ CREE PROPHECY

Introducing: Forest Whitlow

My name is Forest Whitlow. I am Onkwehonwe of the Mohawk Nation from Six Nations of the Grand River Territory. I am 13 years old and in grade eight. My hobbies include dirt bike riding and lacrosse. My main interests right now are females. My favourite kind of music is rap and, in particular, Native rap, i.e., Tru Rez Crew (from Six Nations). This year, I also spend time at the Six Nations Reclamation Site when I can get there.!

Were you born into your spiritual practice or did you convert?

Yes. I attended Long House in my early years. I learn every day.

Briefly describe your home and family.

I live with my mom, step-dad and little brother. We have a dalmation named Jack. We live in our own house, which could be described as being in the country.

For you, what would make a great weekend?

A great weekend would be hanging out with friends, having a camp-out that included go-carts and laser tag.

What worries or concerns you about the world or your life these days?

Things that concern me would be losing a family member or failing in school. I am also concerned about drug houses in our community. Racism is a problem, especially since the incidents at the Reclamation Site in the town of Caledonia. I worry about things going down at the Reclamation Site that would cause harm to our people. I've been there and heard non-Natives yelling out, "Get a job!" "Go home!" "****ing dirty Indians!" and "Give us back our four-wheelers!" I don't appreciate being called a terrorist or an Indian.

Where do you learn the stories and traditions of your spirituality?

This year I am spending time at the Six Nations Reclamation Site when I can get there. I learn about stories and our way of being by listening to the old ones, the Elders, and the teachings at the Reclamation Site.

In what ways do you think your tradition helps you live your life?

My spiritual tradition teaches me that being Onkwehonwe, we are the original people of this land. We are not extinct. We are a proud culture and would like the world to understand that we remain sovereign.

My spiritual path requires keeping a good mind and the teachings of the Great Law.[2] I am guided to follow the path of Peace, Power, and Righteousness.

What two or three things would you like people to know about your religion?

I would like people to know three things about the Haudenosaunee:[3] we're not extinct; we're not Indians; and we are proud of who we are. I think that Canada needs a real history lesson. I think that understanding could come through listening to each other.

A Prayer for Healing[4]

Grandfather,

Look at our brokenness.

We know that in all creation
Only the human family
Has strayed from the Sacred Way.
We know that we are the ones
And we are the ones
Who must come back together
Who are divided
To walk in the Sacred Way.

Grandfather,
Sacred One,
Teach us love, compassion
*   and honour*
That we may heal the Earth
And heal each other.

~ Elder Arthur Solomon

The Medicine Wheel

The sacred circle, also called the medicine wheel, is extremely important in Aboriginal culture and holds within its shape many ancient teachings. It represents completion and the roundness of Earth. Each of the four directions on the wheel is represented by a colour:

A Story of Aboriginal Spirituality

There is no one Aboriginal spirituality and no one leader. The Aborigines of Australia, the Masai of East Africa and the Blackfoot of western Canada and the United States, for example, all developed their own distinctive art, beliefs, rites and rituals. The west coast Haida are known for their totem poles, but totem poles are not part of the practice of the Blackfoot. Their dances, stories and songs also differ from those of the other nations. It is not possible to write about all the rich variety of traditions even on Turtle Island (North America); at the time of

Thumbnail Sketch

Who is the founder? There is no one founder. This spirituality evolved over time in all parts of the world. Some of the wisdom and teachings of spiritual leaders, such as Black Elk of the Sioux and Chief Dan George of the Salish, have been left to us on paper and can be found in friendship centres, universities, and public libraries.

When did it start? In the beginning; tens of thousands of years ago.

red, white, black or blue, and yellow. Each direction holds powerful teachings. For example, east represents illumination; south is trust; west represents introspection; and the north represents wisdom.[5] The four directions can also represent the four seasons or the four races of humanity. Medicine wheels can be seen today on lapel buttons (called unity buttons because they symbolize the four races of humans), at sacred sites, and even in satellite photos of ancient stone formations created generations ago. There are many large stone medicine wheels across the west in both Canada and the United States. One of the best-known is the Big Horn medicine wheel in Wyoming. It is nearly 30 m (100 ft.) across.

European contact (1492), there were almost 50 different language and cultural groups thriving there.

However, there are amazing similarities among many tribes, not only on Turtle Island, but all around the world. For example, when Cree Elder Myra Laramee travelled from Winnipeg, Canada, to Udaipur, India, and met tribal people there, she found their worldview much the same as hers and was surprised to learn that the bear, a symbol of power and healing, was viewed the same way by both tribes.

Generally speaking, indigenous peoples have traditionally respected and honoured the Earth. Sacred rituals performed around the world point to this reverence and respect for the cycles of life. Examples include prayers before and after a hunt, and those offered before planting as well as at harvest time. Rituals such as the vision quest also honour the season of a young person's life. Respect for older people is also common among many peoples worldwide. In some modern societies, older people are not considered valuable,

Are there any foundational sacred texts? Earth, water, air, fire, animals – all life is viewed as sacred and something to learn from. The rites, ceremonies, and stories were and are passed on orally.

In what places do people worship? In sacred groves of trees, by sacred fires, on mountaintops, also in long houses, round houses, lodges, kivas, tipis and in people's homes – anywhere.

What are worship leaders called? Elders, shamans, medicine people, or holy people.

Where is the tradition practised? Wherever Aboriginal people live.

Are there special holy days? Every day is considered holy, particularly summer and winter solstice, full moon, new moon, and other days determined by the community and their particular history.

Mountain Woman

Asanee Watchew Iskwiw, Mountain Woman (also known as Lorraine Sinclair), was a Cree cultural teacher and spiritual leader. She spent much of her life learning the ceremonies and teachings of Elders such as Eddie Bellerose, Chief Robert Smallboy, Tom Badger, and Norbert Jebeaux. She travelled to Britain and, through a vision there, understood that the history of all peoples is connected, just like humans and the Great Spirit are connected to Earth.

In 1988, Mountain Woman began to share the teachings of the wise ones with Native and non-Native people. Mountain Woman knew that one of the greatest needs of the world was the healing of the planet and so she began an organization called The Mother Earth Healing Society, which is dedicated to the preservation and healing of Earth through the

but in traditional indigenous societies, the teachings of Elders are important. Elders are the ones who carry the oral history of the people and teach the rituals and ceremonies. People go to them for advice, healing and help resolving conflicts. Today, Elders are invited into schools to share stories and their knowledge. Children too are valued, so much that in some traditions, such as the Six Nations, decisions are made based on what would be best for the seventh generation, meaning the great, great, great grandchildren of the next generation. Most indigenous peoples also value and share responsibility for the welfare of the whole community, rather than take an individualistic, competitive approach. Black Elk, an Oglala Sioux prophet and holy man, taught that we are all connected to one another: animal beings, the Great Spirit, and Earth.

Aboriginal teachings and practices have not always been respected the way they are today. When the first European explorers arrived on Turtle Island, they brought missionaries who tried to convert the populations already living here. Much of the land

Words to Know

Aboriginal: existing before the arrival of colonists. Aboriginal typically means Inuit, Metis, Native American and First Nations peoples.

Fast: to stop eating (and sometimes drinking). People fast as a spiritual discipline, to help focus on prayer and meditation. Fasting may also be part of a ceremony or ritual of thanksgiving, to pay homage, to make a gift or sacrifice.

First Nations: The nations living in North America before the colonists arrived.

Indigenous: "of the land" or having originated in a particular environment.

teachings of Native cultural values. She was the fire keeper there, and she held talking circles that were open to people of all nations. She also travelled far and wide to speak with people open to her message, to learn from other teachers, and to work with school students and troubled youth in order to help them learn the ways of the ancestors, and to encourage them to live in a good way.

that indigenous peoples occupied was gradually taken over by the settlers. In North America, many First Nations children were sent to schools run by the government and religious organizations. The children were not allowed to speak in their native languages, to participate in their traditional ceremonies, or to learn about their own heritage and culture. In many cases, they were abused by the people who administered these schools. The pain and distress caused by this residential school system, which operated in Canada from 1874 into the 1970s, is still felt today.

Aboriginal spirituality is no longer suppressed. For many Native people today, it provides a way to heal the abuses of the past. It also has much to teach non-Native people, particularly in terms of how to care for Earth. Earth is viewed as sacred mother because she feeds us and provides everything we need to live. To care for Earth is

Kiva: a room for religious ritual, especially in the kachina belief system in the American Southwest.

Nation: a group of Aboriginal people with common ancestry.

Tribe: see definition for nation.

Vision or Spirit Quest: a period of spiritual seeking, (often at puberty), that typically involves isolation, fasting, meditation, prayer.

The Seventh Generation

Many indigenous traditions speak about the seventh generation, referring to ways of making responsible decisions so that all those who come after us, down to seven generations, will not have to clean up our messes or suffer. Keeping the planet healthy, the rivers clean and the air pure are examples of this kind of thinking, as are telling stories and keeping the culture alive. Today, some companies have taken this message to heart. Some produce recycled, non-chlorinated paper for computer printers, for example, so that fewer trees will die and rivers won't be polluted. Some companies even call themselves Seventh Generation.

Rituals and Ceremonies

to care for ourselves. This means it is important not to waste food, cause pollution, or take more than we need.

To learn more about Aboriginal spiritual practices, you might begin by visiting a cultural centre or friendship centre and asking to speak with a cultural teacher or Elder. You may learn about a gathering to attend or about a weekend retreat open to people from all nations.

People in ceremonies generally sit in a circle, often on the ground. There may be a fire in the middle or a candle, a medicine bundle, a sacred pipe and/or special symbols the Elder carries. The circle allows people to see and hear one another and to know their faces and gestures when and if they speak. The Elder and his or her helper often walk around the circle and offer the smudge to the people gathered. After each person has washed themselves with the smoke and offered a silent prayer, the Elder gives a teaching. The Elder may then pass a talking stick, rock, or eagle feather around the circle, beginning on his or her left so that the movement is clockwise, following the movement of the sun.

As participants hold the item, they have the attention of the whole group and are free to speak from their heart. No one interrupts the person speaking, comments, or asks a question other than the Elder. After the person finishes speaking, he or she passes the item on to the next person. People are free to pass on the item without speaking, if they wish. When the item returns to the Elder, more prayers are offered. There may also be drumming and singing.

The hand drum is common in most Aboriginal cultures and is used in religious or spiritual ceremonies. The drum represents the heart beat of Mother Earth. Its round shape represents the circle of life.

The Peacemaker and the Tree of Peace

Long ago, there was a special boy, of the Huron nation on Turtle Island, who thought hard about how people lived, and dreamed that there must be a better way than war to solve problems. When he grew up, he had a dream of peace. He meditated on this dream and in time had a vision of democracy and uni-ty. He visualized a tree to represent his dream. The branches of the tree offered shelter. The roots held the tree firm in Mother Earth.

The Peace-maker, as he became known, began searching for someone to help him work for peace among the nations. He looked every-where, including in the Onondaga nation, the Huron nation's enemy. Eventually, he found a great speaker he believed could help him. But the man was in mourning for his wife and daughters. They had recently been mur-

Smudging

A sacred medicine or herb burns in a container, such as a large sea shell or a bowl made of pottery or metal. The Elder or helper pick the medicine during a prayerful gathering; it might be diamond willow fungus, sweet grass, tobacco, cedar, or sage. Some-one fans the medicine, often with an eagle feather, to keep it smoking. The smoke in a smudge, like the smoke from incense or a ceremonial pipe, rises to symbolically carry prayers to the Creator and into the Spirit world.

When the smudge is brought to a person, he or she usually removes eye glasses, watch, and jewellery, washes him or herself with the smoke and offers a silent prayer. At Niji Mahkwa School in Winnipeg, Manitoba, the children are taught that when they smudge they should try to be mindful of the following:

We smudge to clear the air around us.

We smudge our minds in order to have good thoughts of others.

We smudge our eyes in order to be able to see the good in others.

We smudge our ears so that we will only listen to good things about others.

dered, and he was deep in grief. His name was Hiawatha.

People believed that Hiawatha would rather seek revenge than sit around talking. The Huron and Onondaga nations had been enemies for years. But the people were wrong. In spite of everything, Hiawatha sat down and listened. He listened and be- lieved in the vision of peace.

Hiawatha left his home and joined the Peacemaker. For five years the two men travelled from nation to nation, village to village, offering hope for an end to fighting and ideas for ways to live in peace.

In 1390 CE, the Mohawk, Ononda- ga, Seneca, Cayuga, and Oneida nations came together and declared peace. Later, the Tuscaro- ras joined, making the union known as The Six Nations Confederacy. With the help of the clan mothers, the wisest and most noble men were named to help create a democratic and peaceful society. The council created The Law of the Great Peace of the People of the Long House (also known as the Great Law of Peace).

As a symbol of this new peace, the warriors buried their hatchets, or war clubs, in a deep hole. Over these weapons they planted a great white pine, the tree of peace.

To this day, the people gather and read aloud the constitution created hundreds of years ago. To this day, there is also peace among the nations of the confederacy. People still plant a tree of peace as a symbol of hope, peace, and new beginnings. And people from many nations all around the world continue to learn about the Six Nations Confed- eracy, the Tree of Peace, and the Law of the Great Peace.

We smudge our heart so that we will only feel good about our life with others. We smudge our whole being so that we may portray the good part of our self through our actions."[6]

The Sweat Lodge

The sweat lodge is also known to many people. From the Arctic coast to South America, the sweat lodge has been used for many centuries. It is similar to a Turkish bath, Finnish sauna, and Roman bath, in that water is poured on hot rocks to produce steam, and people sit in the dark to sweat. In addition to cleaning oneself, people from many traditions also go into a sweat lodge with a spiritual motive. People who enter a sweat lodge undergo a purification process.

Although there are varia- tions in how the lodge is created (for example, it may be like a small, curved tent made of canvas over bent willows, or it may be made from mud bricks) the sweat lodge is usually offered by an Elder who invites participants into it as if to pray. Entering the dark round lodge is seen as entering the womb of Mother Earth. The Elder prays and perhaps uses a ceremonial object, such

as a hand drum or rattle. Sometimes people see visions in the lodge or they may sense the presence of the ancestors. Outside, a fire keeper stokes the fire with a supply of hot rocks and keeps watch over the lodge.

As with many other sacred rituals, the sweat lodge ceremony was attacked by settlers new to North America. They did not understand what it was and were afraid of it. Today, some non-Natives have learned about the value of this spiritual practice and have been invited to participate in a sweat lodge ceremony.

Menstruation

In some traditions, like the Lakota Sioux, menstruating women withdraw to a menstrual hut to be quiet during this purification time. Some women today would love to be able to withdraw from their busy lives a few days a month.

Sun Dance Ceremony

The Sun Dance is a sacred ceremony practised by prairie nations and others for centuries. It was outlawed at one time by the settler societies that came to North America, but there is a great revival of the dance today. There are variations in the way the Sun Dance is performed, and about 20 different tribes on Turtle Island perform it. It is performed around the time of the summer solstice, with attention to the phases of the moon. A special tree is chosen to stand in the centre of the dance circle, to hold such offerings as pouches of tobacco and to hold the tether that will eventually be attached to the dancers.

People prepare for a whole year before they dance. They learn from an Elder or mentor; they meditate and pray to get ready for this sacred ritual. The community surrounds and supports the people who will dance, fast, and pray for four days. Dancers dance for bravery, generosity, inner strength, and integrity. At the end of the four days, the community celebrates with a feast.

Rites of Passage

There are many different rites and rituals. They are usually centred around a life transition and are often traditional in the particular culture.

Vision or Spirit Quest

A vision quest is first taken from about the age of 12 up through the teens, though it can take place at any age. The seeker speaks with the spiritual leader about this important step, and the leader helps to prepare the person with instruction, story and prayer. In some traditions, the person goes into the sweat lodge and prays. The leader takes the seeker to a secluded place and gives instructions about how long to stay there and how to listen for the guidance of the Great Spirit. The seeker fasts and watches, listens and prays. The seeker may see visions and gain understanding from the ancestors, the spirit world and the natural world that helps him or her discover more about who they are.

The quest is a challenge of strength and courage. The seeker usually learns his or her place in the community and also who his or her guardian spirit is. Boys go on a vision quest; in some nations girls do this also.

Girl's Puberty Ceremony

There are different ceremonies for girls in different nations. One tradition is practised today by the Apache. When a girl begins menstruation, the family and community celebrate, sometimes for up to 12 days.[7] The ceremony, which includes blessings and sacred rituals, helps to honour and connect the girl to her spiritual heritage and to the creation story of White Painted Woman (also called Changing Woman). The girl hears how White Painted Woman gave birth to the world and taught ceremonies, rituals, and how to use medicines. When White Painted Woman became old, she walked east toward the rising sun and was reborn, reminding everyone that the world is always being renewed and changing. Singing, praying, gift giving and storytelling are all part of honouring the girl-becoming-woman.

Notes

[1] The Six Nations Reclamation Site is an area near the town of Caledonia, Ontario, which the Six Nations people are reclaiming. In 2006, the Six Nations of the Grand River found themselves in a standoff with police and government officials supporting the development of a housing subdivision on the site. Some clashes also occurred with the residents of Caledonia. The land in question was part of an agreement made in 1784 between the Council of Chiefs of the Haudenosaunee and the British government.

[2] The Great Law of Peace was given to the Haudenosaunee by Hiawatha and the Peacemaker. (See sidebar on the Peacemaker in this chapter.) The Great Law is the founding constitution of the Six Nations Iroquois Confederacy. It defines the functions of the Grand Council and how the Native nations of the confederacy can resolve disputes between themselves and maintain peace. Refer to the following Web site for more information: http://sixnations.buffnet.net/Great_Law_of_Peace/

[3] Haudenosaunee means "people building a Long House." The Long House is a way of life where the Cayuga, Mohawk, Oneida, Onondaga, Seneca and Tuscarora nations live in peace under one common law. In English, the Haudenosaunee were also referred to as The Six Nations or Iroquois Confederacy.

[4] Arthur Solomon, *Songs of the People: Teachings on the Natural Way* (Toronto: New Canada Publications, 1990).

[5] Citizens for Public Justice (brochure), Toronto.

[6] Used with permission of Myra Laramee, principal at Niji Mahkwa School.

[7] Joel W. Martin, *The Land Looks After Us: A History of Native American Religion* (New York: Oxford University Press, 2001), p. 116. See also: http://www.webwinds.com/yupanqui/apachesunrise.htm

Golden Rule

All things are our relatives; what
we do to every thing, we do to
ourselves. All is really One.

~ BLACK ELK, OGLALA SIOUX
(1863–1950)

Chapter 3

Hinduism

Green Rule

I am the fragrance of the Earth,

the heat in fire.

I am the life of all that lives.

~ Bhagavad Gita 7.9

Introducing: Ramya Gopal

My name is Ramya Gopal and I was born into Hinduism. I live in an ordinary suburb of Detroit with both my parents. But I will reside in a college dormitory next year, coming back home for the holidays. I will be a freshman at Swarthmore College.

Aside from school, I spend some of my time combining writing with activism as well as pursuing more artistic hobbies, such as studying vocal Carnatic music [Indian classical music] and Bharthnatyam dance [Indian classical dance]. These last two years, I also served as a student representative on a board of the city of Troy.

For you, what would make a great weekend?

For me, every weekend is a great weekend simply because I can take time away from the routine of school. My family usually prays at the temple every Saturday morning, and the weekend is usually a time to spend with the family. Going out with friends can turn a great weekend into a perfect weekend.

What worries or concerns you about the world or your life these days?

Many of the decisions in this modern era point to a conservative and sometimes regressive swing. I am worried that in our effort to try to protect ourselves from harmful influences, we are forgetting the few truths of equality and understanding that have helped us grow as a civilization. I see it in America's approach to controversial issues such as gay marriage and the clash between the West and the Middle East. I do sometimes see it in my own life too, pushing away ideas that seem to conflict with my way of living, but I've learned that keeping an open mind is important.

Where do you learn the stories and traditions of your religion?

When we went to India in the summers, my parents would buy me comic books called "Amar Chitra Katha," which would depict certain religious stories, and my father would read them to me every night when I was a child. For many years, I took part in a type of Hindu religion class called "Balavihar" where we would learn all the stories, the mantras, the basic "Advaita" philosophy, the traditions and ceremonies for holidays and various pujas. This way, I became knowledgeable in the practical and theoretical aspects of Hinduism. More recently, I have been a part of Navya Shastra, the Hindu reform organization that works for human rights. There, I learned about scholars like V. V. Raman, whose writings help explain some of the philosophical aspects of Hinduism.

In what ways do you think your tradition helps you live your life?

It has changed over the years, as the challenges I face have evolved. "Ramayana" and the "Mahabharata" (the two most important Hindu epics) depict characters of valour and nobility, and I have always tried to emulate their pristine characteristics. These virtues include respect towards parents, steadfastness and dedication, honesty, purity of the mind and character; these are all part of the stories and values of Hinduism. I re-read the stories every now and then to keep me in check. I use the morals of the stories to guide me to be a compassionate, trustworthy person. As a child, I would pray when I was afraid of the dark. I still pray, but because I am afraid of bigger things. It's comforting to look beyond the mortal world for protection.

Are there ways that your religion is a problem for you?

Unfortunately, Hinduism isn't perfect. There is one ceremony, called "Upanayanm" (which means "living near God"), that conflicts with my ideals. It celebrates a child's spiritual maturity into adulthood, when the child begins the journey of spiritual and religious education. This ceremony, however, is only for upper-caste boys. However, I have tried to not stand by and just let this custom continue. A few years ago, I wrote an article illuminating this problem and illustrating some ways in which to change it. On the other hand, I am glad that there is at least a somewhat parallel ceremony for girls called "Ritu Kala Samskara" (which means "coming-of-age ceremony").

Does your religion have anything special to say to teens or children?

Many (of the) stories are directed towards children, or (at the very least) are simplified for children. I built a foundation of knowledge of my religion as well as a foundation of believing, which has remained with me. I have known some Hindus of my generation who have never had this chance, thus, losing a connection to a structured religion.

Have you ever been (or would you like to be) part of an interfaith event, worship or action?

I hope to be involved with interfaith events in college.

People have talked often about what divides people who practise different religions. What do you think could bring (or is bringing) religious people together?

In "Androcles and the Lion" by George Bernard Shaw, Lavinia tells the Captain that she gets along very well with people of any religion, because they believe sincerely. "Religion is such a great thing that when I meet really religious people we are friends at once, no matter what name we give to the Divine that made us and moves us." Although the play was written a century ago in a different context, I think the message still rings true today. Despite the ritualistic and historical differences, the philosophical basis for all religions is the same, and I think we need to remember that more often.

What is your wish for the youth of the world?

The world has become inextricably interconnected, and I hope that our generation will embrace this so we can learn to understand each other better. I also hope that more of us will share the burden of civic duty in the ways of volunteering, being knowledgeable in the problems of the world, so the growing co-operation will lead to greater success in the future. In terms of religion, I hope that we can set aside our differences. In the words of the Hindu scholar, Professor V. V. Raman, "My own hope [is] that all religions would learn from one another to improve themselves, and live in harmony."

Do you have any advice for religious or other leaders in the world today?

All leaders were once young and idealistic (some still are), and I'd advise them to not forget the idealism that created religious institutions, regardless of the politics that soil it. The most important value to remember, I believe, is accepting and appreciating all traditions.

What two or three things would you like people to know about your religion?

Karma and rebirth are two complex ideas that are unique to Indic traditions, including Hinduism. Karma refers to the principle that no one can escape the consequences of one's actions. Rebirth is the belief that one will be born again to reap the consequences of one's actions in a previous birth. Also unique to Hinduism is the explicit tolerance of other religions and other strands of our religion. Despite the differences in our denominations (which god or goddess one worships), we celebrate the religious and cultural holidays together.

A Prayer for Peace[1]

Oh God, lead us from the

unreal to the Real.

Oh God, lead us from darkness to light.

Oh God, lead us from death to immortality.

Shanti, Shanti, Shanti unto all.

Oh Lord God almighty, may there be peace in

celestial regions.

May there be peace on Earth.

May the waters be appeasing.

May herbs be wholesome, and may trees and

plants bring peace to all. May all beneficent

beings bring peace to us.

May thy Vedic Law propagate peace all

through the world.

May all things be a source of peace to us.

And may thy peace itself, bestow peace on all

and may that peace come to me also.

~Swami Omkar

Hindu Stories and Poems

Ramayana and Mahabharata are story-poems that have lasted hundreds of years and are still performed, sung, and danced. Ramayana is the story of Rama, his life and his love for Sita. Like all good stories, it teaches values for living through a series of dramatic incidents that include love and war, birth and death, and defeat and rescue.

At one time in Indian history, kings believed themselves to be above the law, but Ramayana set a new model for all to follow. This story of Sita and Rama teaches respect, justice and loyalty.

A Story of Hinduism

One of the distinguishing characteristics of Hinduism today is that it is open to many different religious ideas. That is why there are so many goddesses and gods – people are free to choose one that will help them. That is also why many Hindus feel comfortable stopping by a church or other religious building to pray. Hinduism is not so much about correct belief as it is about a way of life. The religion is actually an abundance of beliefs and

Thumbnail Sketch

Who is the founder? There is no one founder.

When did it start? Around 5000 BCE.

Are there any foundational sacred texts? The Vedas, Upanishads, epic poems, Dharma Shastras, and Puranas.

In what places do people worship? In temples, at home, at holy rivers, forest groves and roadside shrines.

What are worship leaders called? Brahmins (priests), sadhus (holy men), gurus (teachers) or pandits (learned ones).

Where is the tradition practised? Mainly in India; worldwide.

Mahabharata is a sacred story-poem, said to be the longest in the world with 100,000 verses! It tells of the end of one era and the beginning of another, a great triumph of good over evil. The Bhagavad-Gita is a famous and loved part of the Mahabharata. This epic tells the history of Indian Hindu mythology, philosophy, state governance, social order, values, beliefs and views. It teaches other things too, such as selfless duty and living a God-centred life.

Bhagavad-Gita means "song of the Lord." The story tells how Lord Krishna came to earth to fight evil. In the story, Krishna meets Arjuna, a warrior prince, and convinces him to follow his destiny. Krishna teaches Arjuna that the soul cannot die. He also teaches him that there are three paths people can take to release their soul from the cycle of reincarnation. The three paths are knowledge, good deeds and devotion to a god or goddess.

These stories have been passed down through the generations because they teach important lessons in living.

traditions rather than a single, unified set of beliefs.[2]

Reincarnation is important to Hindus. This concept teaches that when beings die, their souls do not die but are born again in another body. This idea is made visual in the great Wheel of Life that is carved on temples and painted or stitched into works of art. A wheel also appears on the flag of India. Brahma, the creator god, Vishnu, the preserver god, and Shiva, the destroyer, keep the wheel turning endlessly.

Hinduism began in India in the mists of time, some say 5,000 years ago. By around 1500 BCE, the tradition became more organized, that is, leaders selected important stories to teach, decided on rules for right behaviour, and began

What are the main branches of the tradition? There are many gods and goddesses in Hinduism, but Hindus generally follow one of four deities: Vishnu, the affirmer god who sustained the universe and ruled it like a king, with justice, mercy and compassion; Shiva, Lord of the Dance, the destroyer and regenerative god whose dance keeps the universe in motion; Ganesh, the elephant-headed god of new beginnings; or Shakti, the Great Goddess, who is the feminine image of the Supreme Being, the Creator. Her symbol is the downward triangle (womb), and she is the mother of all gods, deities, and Earth beings.

Are there special holy days? Dasarah, Navaratri and Diwali (which is distinct from the Sikh festival of the same name) are associated with the worship of Shakti and the legend of Lord Rama (who is the human form of Vishnu). There are also special celebrations and festivals celebrating Shiva, Ganaptai, Rama and Krishna. Holy days and festivals are based in mythology or on the harvest in spring and autumn. The Hindu calendar is lunar.

Yoga, Fasting and Vegetarianism

Yoga is both a spiritual and physical set of exercises that help people meditate, relieve stress and concentrate on union with the Divine. As with most Hindu teachings, yoga provides many different ways to practise. There are many yoga studios and ashrams open to anyone with the desire to learn.

Some Hindus fast weekly, monthly or during special holy days. Others fast when they feel the need to cleanse and rejuvenate their bodies, spirits and minds. There are many different ways to fast: some people may drink a little water, tea or juice;

writing down prayers. The Sanskrit language (still considered sacred) and the caste system began during this time.

The caste system organized society into four groups: the priests and teachers; the warriors, who were also responsible for governing; the business class; and the servants. Depending on your caste, your marriage partner, career, clothing and educational opportunities were all decided for you. Parts of this system still remain today although human rights groups are working to ensure that people in the lowest caste, who were once called "untouchables," gain their full rights under law. *Dalits* (which translates as "oppressed"), suffered in the past and continue to suffer segregation, violence and racism. Although in parts of India the caste system is still in place, in many parts of the world some people do not pay attention to it.

Around this time, the holy scriptures, the Vedas and the Books of Law were written and refined. Two important epics were also written which are

Words to Know

Ashram: a retreat place, often where people go to learn from a guru.

Brahma: the creator god.

Brahman: the Supreme Spirit, who is formless and incomprehensible and without a beginning or end – everlasting. Goddesses and gods such as Lakshmi (goddess of good fortune, serenity and beauty), Saraswati (goddess of language, music, art and wisdom) and Ganesh illustrate different qualities of brahman.

Caste system: the organization of society into four distinct classes. See "A Story of Hinduism" in this chapter.

Dharma: the Way (of life).

Dharma Shastras: rules for right living.

Ganges River: the most revered of all Indian rivers. According to tradition, the river goddess Ganga flows out of the god Shiva's hair. Orthodox Hindus believe the water is divinely pure. They bathe in and drink it; after cremation, their ashes are scattered in it.

Karma: the law of cause and effect; the belief that people are responsible for their own destiny.

Mantra: a word or sound repeated to help concentrate during meditation.

Nirvana: union with Brahman; release from having to be reincarnated or born again.

others may take a little food or no food at all. Prayer is usually part of the fast.

The two main reasons that Hindus practise vegetarianism are to follow the principle of not killing and to live a healthier lifestyle. There are dozens of magazines and books available in public libraries and health food stores about the health benefits of vegetarianism for humans and for Earth (including animals!). These resources often include articles and recipes as well as information about the health benefits of practising yoga. Fasting is also a growing trend as people look for ways to care for their spirits and bodies. Not all Hindus practise vegetarianism.

still read today: *Ramayana* and the *Mahabharata*.

By 600 BCE, Hindus had developed yoga, a disciplined practice of meditation and breath control. Many people today learn about Hinduism through this discipline, and there are ashrams all around North America. Men wanting to devote themselves solely to spiritual matters built monasteries during this period, and went there to study and meditate. The Upanishads were written in this period. These are the teachings of the Hindu wise people about Brahman, reincarnation, and the nature of creation. They helped people understand more about the Supreme Spirit.

It was also during this period that two men were born into the warrior caste whose lives still impact the world today. They protested against some of the teachings of the day, especially the caste system and animal sacrifice as part of religious worship.

The first of these men was Vardhaman (599–527 BCE), who was known later as *Mahavira*, which means "Great Hero." He was the last of the 24 Great

Om: the Sanskrit symbol for the Divine; the sound of the Divine, used in meditation and prayer.

Puja: worship.

Puranas: collection of Hindu mythological literature.

Reincarnation: the belief that the soul does not die with the body, but is born or incarnated again and again.

Sacred Cow: because Indians receive such kindness from the cow (in the form of milk, cheese, yoghurt and, through cow dung, cooking fuel), cows came to be considered sacred. They are still protected animals in India today.

Shakti: the goddess (or god) of creative energy.

Veda: knowledge; the Vedas are a collection of holy writings that contain ancient knowledge.

Vedic: ancient Hindu wisdom.

Upanishads: part of the Vedic literature, containing discussion about the nature of God, the process of creation and relationships.

Wheel of Life: a visual symbol of reincarnation (birth, life, death and rebirth).

The Gandhi Institute for Nonviolence

When he was a child in South Africa, Arun Gandhi was beaten up both by black people, because they thought he was too white, and by white people, because they thought he was too black. It was a hard way for a boy to learn about the power of non-violence, but from those experiences and from the teachings of his grandfather, Mahatma Gandhi, Arun did learn. He has devoted his life to teaching nonviolence.

The Gandhi

Teachers of the Jain religion. He left his family to become a wandering ascetic and monk. He believed that enlightenment was possible if people would meditate and give up worldly worries, such as wearing clothes. It is said that he wore the same clothes for one year and, when that outfit wore out, he went naked. He brought order to Jainism and is seen as the most important person in establishing the religion.

The second of these influential men was Siddhartha Gautama (563–483 BCE), who was born and raised a prince. When he realized that life held not only pleasure, but disease, old age and death, he too left his family and became a monk. Years later, he became an enlightened being. He became the Buddha. (Read more about him in Chapter 5.)

When these new movements began, they created a reformation of the Hindu teachings. Animal sacrifice stopped. Hindus began building temples for worship, non-violence became a goal, and vegetarianism became more accepted.

Around 1200 CE, Muslim Arab traders and invaders arrived in India impacting Hindu religious practices. Religious practice became more rigid in response to the newcomers and their ideas; people fought for economic and political control. There were attempts at cross-religious understanding, especially in the 1600s, when Sufi (Muslim) mystics and Bhakti (Hindu) mystics shared ideas and learned from each other. But the dialogue between Muslims and Hindus in India has been interrupted many times by ignorance and terrible violence.

In 1869, one of the greatest peacemakers the world has ever known was born. His name was Gandhi. Hi

Institute for Non-violence was established 1991 by Arun and Sunanda, who is his wife as well as a nurse, writer and lecture-partner. Money from the sale of some of Mahatma Gandhi's personal letters provided the funds to begin the institute. The money has enabled the couple to help people around the world to educate for a non-violent future. For most of the year, the Gandhis give lectures to adults, children and youth. You can learn more by contacting the institute at the Christian Brothers University in Memphis, Tennessee, or visiting <u>www.gandhiinstitute.org</u>.

became Mahatma Gandhi. His long life was given to working for justice, racial and religious harmony, and peaceful non-violent change. He brought the British Empire to a standstill when he humbly and simply began a walk for peace to free his beloved India from its colonial rule. In more modern times, John Lennon of England, Martin Luther King, Jr. of the United States, and Chief Ovide Mercredi of Canada studied Gandhi's methods for non-violent change.

Gandhi, a lawyer, was one of the most important thinkers in the world. Deeply religious, he had great knowledge and respect for the truth of all religions. He studied law in England then devoted himself to working for human rights in Africa and in India. He wrote books and travelled widely. He fasted often, as a means of applying political pressure and as a prayer for peace. Today, Arun Gandhi, Mahatma's grandson, and his wife Sunanda carry on the work for peace through the Gandhi Institute for Nonviolence in Memphis, Tennessee.

Gandhi's great challenge was trying to bring peace between Muslims and Hindus. When India gained independence from Britain in 1947, Pakistan and India became separate countries. Most people who live in Pakistan are Muslim.

Another Hindu whose work has gone far beyond the borders of India is the poet and Nobel Prize winner Rabindranath Tagore (1861–1961). Although he lived during the same turbulent times as Gandhi, Tagore's contribution to peace is different. In Bengali and English, Tagore wrote about his

personal faith in ways that non-Hindus could relate to and could learn from.

Maharishi Mahesh Yogi has had a great influence on the West. Born in India in 1917 (and still living in the Netherlands in 2006), Maharishi created a form of yoga practice that he calls Transcendental Meditation, which he brought to the United States and Europe in the 1970s. His program has trained tens of thousands of people to meditate. Partly because many Hollywood stars and pop singers took his courses, the practice spread quickly. Another reason for the popularity of the Maharishi's program is that he made the practice easy to understand for Westerners. He promoted it as a spiritual practice that would help physical and emotional health too.

Gandhi said, "We must be the change we want to see in the world." The one thing about Hinduism that has been true from the very beginning is that it is always changing.

Hindus have many different rites of passage for births, marriages and deaths. These rituals are influenced by the cultural practices of people, depending on where they live.

Rituals for Babies

Some rituals may be performed for a baby before it is even born. During pregnancy, parents can say prayers for the health of the baby; a father-to-be may brush his wife's hair in a special way as part of a prayer ritual too. After the child has been born, the father can perform other rituals seeking health and long life for the babe. Ceremonies can be performed by family for the naming of the baby (usually when the child is 12 days old), for its first feeding of solid food (around six months) and at a boy's first haircut (around one year old). Traditionally, the baby's first visit outside the home is to the temple.

Marriage

Many marriages are arranged by the parents of the bride and groom, perhaps with the help of a matchmaker. The bride and groom may meet only a few times before they are married and not know each other at all. These marriages have roughly the same rate of survival as western-style love matches. Horoscopes may be cast for the bride and groom in order to determine the best time for the wedding. Of course, Hindus in India or elsewhere follow different customs and conventions. Not all marriages are arranged. Some are love matches. Other couples might be introduced and gently urged to marry, but in the end the decision belongs to the couple.

Puja

In Hindu homes, whether in India or North America, a room or corner is set aside for the puja. Puja may take place every morning or afternoon, or in the evening, or both. It can involve prayers to goddesses or gods and body movements as well. The area is decorated with paintings or statues of favourite goddesses or gods. There is incense as well as bowls for offerings, such as rice or flowers. There may be a photo of a relative who has died. There will likely be a rug on which to kneel and pray. The mother of the family usually has responsibility for the puja. Puja is also given in public places, such as river banks or at temples.

Rites of Passage

Upanayanam In the priestly caste, when a boy approaches puberty, his family may welcome him into the adult religious life with a "twice-born" (coming-of-age) ceremony. This will mark the beginning of the boy's religious and social education. In this ceremony, the boy recites prayers and sacred scripture, and the family priest gives the boy a sacred thread to be worn over his left shoulder as a reminder of the rite. He will recite a mantra that he is meant to say every day for the rest of his life.

Ritu Kala Samskara In traditional families, a girl beginning to menstruate is honoured with a sacrament called the *ritu kala samskara* to welcome her into womanhood. The ceremony recognizes the physical development of the girl and also her emotional and spiritual growth. The ritu kala is attended only by women who sing and may give the girl gifts. On this occasion, she receives her first sari.

Notes
1 From: http://www.indianchild.com/hindu_prayers.htm
2 This definition can be found at the following Web site: http://hinduism.iskcon.com/tradition/1105.htm

Golden Rule

This is the sum of duty:

do not do to others

what would cause pain

if done to you.

~ MAHABHARATA 5:1517

Chapter 4

Judaism

Green Rule

God led the first human beings around all the trees of the Garden of Eden and said, "See my works, how beautiful and praiseworthy they are! Think of this, and do not corrupt or destroy my world."

~ ECCLESIASTES RABBAH 7

Introducing: Shoshana Wolf

My name is Shoshana Wolf. I am 12 years old in grade eight. I do five types of dance: lyrical, jazz, ballet, pointe and hip hop. I like swimming and reading. I listen to a lot of different types of music.

Were you born into your religion or did you convert?

I was born into Judaism.

Briefly describe your home and family.

I have six people in my family: one sister, two brothers, parents, and two cats. I live in a very nice house. My siblings and I get along and are very close.

For you, what would make a great weekend?

A great weekend would be hanging out with a bunch of my friends, going swimming and having a sleepover with my best friend.

What worries or concerns you about the world or your life these days?

I am concerned for the world environment and all the fighting.

Where do you learn the stories and traditions of your spirituality?

I learn the stories and traditions from my older brother, my dad, and my rabbi.

In what ways do you think your tradition helps you live your life?

My religion has holidays that I celebrate and, in Judaism, there are many guidelines that I must follow.

Are there ways that your religion is a problem for you?

My religion has a dietary restriction, which can be very hard for me at times because there are a lot of things I can't eat, and I feel different from my friends.

Does your religion have anything special to say to teens or children?

I belong to two youth groups: National Conference of Synagogue Youth (NCSY) and Kadima. They are both just fun groups to teach you about Judaism and meet new Jewish friends. It is very fun.

Have you ever been (or would you like to be) part of an interfaith event, worship, or action?

I made a presentation about Miriam at a multifaith event this year. The group is called Women in Spirituality.

People have talked often about what divides people who practise different religions. What do you think could bring (or is bringing) religious people together?

People would come more together if everyone was interested in different religions and took the time to meet people from other religions.

What is your wish for the youth of the world?

I wish the youth of the world would have high morals.

Do you have any advice for religious or other leaders in the world today?

Be accepting of each other's religions.

What two or three things would you like people to know about your religion?

I would like people to know that women are valued in my religion. I would also like people to know that although my religion is demanding, it offers daily focus and guidance.

A Prayer

This prayer is the opening of the Shema, from the book of Deuteronomy (6: 4), and it forms part of religious services.

Hear, O Israel: The Lord is our God;

the Lord is One.

And thou shalt love the Lord

thy God with all thy heart,

with all thy soul and with all thy might.

And these words, which I command

thee this day,

shall be upon thy heart;

and thou shalt teach them

diligently unto thy children.

Women in Judaism

Judaism is a matrilineal religion, meaning that it is through the mother that children receive the right to call themselves Jewish. As in many religions, there are different practices concerning women's responsibilities and opportunities. Although Orthodox Jewish women do not become rabbis, Reform women can. Some women are great teachers. For example, Sandy Eisenberg Sasso has been a rabbi since 1977. She is active in the arts, civic affairs, interfaith communities and has written and lectured on women and spirituality

A Story of Judaism

Judaism is a religion of stories. Hebrew scriptures are filled with intrigue, wild dramas, love, betrayal, and a people struggling to be faithful to God. From the beginning, one key difference between the beliefs of the Hebrews and those of the neighbouring people they clashed with was that the Hebrews believed there is only one God, who created the world and everything in it. The Jews understood that God was involved in their lives and cared about them. From the beginning, too, the people were commanded to tell their stories to the next generations. Whether Jews regularly practise their religion or not, the "People of the

and the religious imagination of children. Rabbi Sasso is famous as the author of children's books such as God's Paintbrush, *A Prayer for the Earth* and *In God's Name*.

In traditional Jewish homes, it is the responsibility of mothers to educate children about the faith and keep the home rituals such as holy-day celebrations and the Sabbath meal. The Sabbath takes place on Saturday but begins at sundown on Friday. Before the Friday evening meal, the woman of the house lights the Sabbath candles and prays. The home is considered the "sanctuary of Israel."

Book" (Torah) are connected to the history of their ancestors through stories.

Avraham (Abraham) and Sarah were an unlikely old couple chosen to journey, lead and take part in a miracle. God told Avraham to pack up his family, servants and flocks and move to Canaan. There, he would become the father of a great nation. This marked the first covenant that God made with the "chosen people" – people chosen for special responsibilities to follow the holy laws. This covenant was sealed with a mark that is honoured even today: Avraham and all men and boys with him were circumcised.

Thumbnail Sketch

Who are the founders? Avraham (Abraham) and Sarah; Moses.

When did it start? About 3000 BCE.

In what places do people worship? In synagogues and at home.

Are there any foundational sacred texts? Torah (The Five Books of Moses), Nevi'im (The Prophets), Kethuvim (The Writings), and the Talmud (writings by rabbis).

What are religious leaders called? Rabbis (teachers) and cantors (who are pastoral and worship leaders).

Where is the tradition practised? Mainly in Israel, North America, South America, Russia and Europe.

What are the main branches of the tradition? Orthodox (the branch that follows the Torah laws more literally), Conservative and Reform (the branch that has a less literal understanding of the Torah).

Are there special holy days? Pesach (also known as Passover) is an eight-day celebration that commemorates when Israelites fled slavery in Egypt. Shavuot celebrates the day the Ten Commandments were received. Sukkot is a pilgrimage feast and eight-day festival of thanksgiving. Purim is one of the most joyous holidays and celebrates the time when good Queen Esther saved her people from extermination; children often perform the story as a play. Rosh Hashanah is the Jewish New Year, a time for remembering the creation of the world. Yom Kippur (Day of Atonement) is the holiest day of the Jewish calendar year; a day of fasting. On this day, Jews ask for forgiveness and forgive others. Most holy days and seasons are designated by verses in the Torah and represent agricultural celebrations. In modern times, moral and historical meanings have been added to these special days. The Jewish calendar is lunar.

Words to Know

Circumcise: to remove the foreskin from the penis.

Covenant: agreement between God and a person or nation.

Hanukkah (or Chanukkah): the eight-day winter Festival of Lights commemorating the time when Jews, after having won a great battle for the freedom to practise their religion, went to the Temple in Jerusalem to celebrate. Even though there was only enough oil to burn the lamp for one day, the lamp burned for eight days.

Hashem: means "the Name." It is used by Jews who consider it rude or offensive to speak God's name. There are many other ways to refer to the Creator, including the Compassionate One, Elohim and Adonai.

Hebrew: another name for Jew.

Israelite: member of the ancient Hebrew nation.

Menorah: a special candle holder used at Hanukkah.

Kosher: food that has been prepared according to Jewish laws. It includes animals that have been killed humanely, bled properly and with prayer, and cooked in an especially clean kitchen. It excludes shellfish, pork, birds of prey and menus where milk and meat are served together. These food laws helped assure proper respect for animals. It also encouraged Jews to share food with their community.

Sabbath: a day for rest and worship. Sabbath begins Friday evening and continues until sundown on Saturday.

Shalom: translates as "peace." It is a Jewish greeting.

Shekinah: means "She who dwells within," and refers to the female presence of God in Jewish tradition.

Temple: the first was built in Jerusalem by King Solomon around 950 BCE and was destroyed in 586 BCE by the Babylonians. It was rebuilt and destroyed again in 70 CE by the Romans. Today, one wall remains, and it is a place of prayer. It is called the Western Wall. Men and women pray separately there.

The Ten Commandments

The Ten Commandments (found in Deuteronomy and Exodus) are but a few of the 613 that were gradually given to Moses over time. The story tells us that these ten were written in stone and begin with the statement, "I am the Lord your God, who brought you out of the land of Egypt, from the house of slavery."

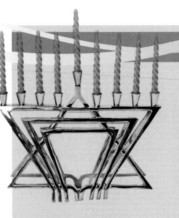

Although Sarah and her husband had longed for children, they were very old and childless. They had given up hope long ago. But one day, angels announced that Sarah would become pregnant. The story tells us that Avraham was about 100 years old and Sarah was 90. Sarah laughed at this absurd idea – at first. They named their son Isaac.

Isaac married Rebekah. Their son Jacob (whom God renamed Israel) had 12 sons. These 12 were the beginning of the 12 Tribes of Israel. Current events today would be quite different if Canaan hadn't experienced drought and severe famine at this time. But the people were driven to leave home so they wouldn't starve to death. They migrated to Egypt under the protection of Joseph, one of the 12 sons, who by

1) Have no other gods besides me.

2) Do not make images or any likeness of what is in the heavens above.

3) Do not use the name of the Lord in vain, or make insincere oaths.

4) Remember to observe the Sabbath day and keep it holy.

5) Honour your mother and father.

6) Do not murder.

7) Do not commit adultery.

8) Do not steal.

9) Do not bear false witness against your neighbour.

10) Do not covet what belongs to your neighbour.

an amazing turn of events had become part of the pharaoh's (the king's) court.

The Hebrews stayed in Egypt for generations, but they did not become like the Egyptians. They continued to follow their own religion. The Egyptians regarded them with suspicion. Around 1300 BCE, a pharaoh (king) took the throne who forgot the story about his ancestor agreeing to protect the Hebrews. He viewed their growing population with alarm. He didn't understand people who would worship only one god. Their customs were different, their language strange. There were too many of them; what if they rose up against him? Eventually, his fear drove him to take away their freedoms bit by bit. When he wanted to expand his empire and needed labourers, he devised a plan. He took their last bit of freedom

and made them slaves. Even though their lives were hard, the Hebrews' allegiance to God remained strong for generations. They believed that, one day, they would be saved.

Ramses II was pharaoh when a crisis began to brew. He became obsessed with the population control of his slaves. He ordered Hebrew midwives to kill boys at birth. He sent soldiers to ensure the order was obeyed. It was not, of course.

One baby boy lived to change history. His mother Jocheved wove a basket, set her baby in it and floated it in the Nile River so that when soldiers checked their shack, they wouldn't find him. His sister Miriam hid on the riverbank, keeping watch. When Pharaoh's daughter arrived at the river

Jewish-Christian Dialogue

After World War II, many Christians woke up to the fact that some interpretations of their scriptures had contributed to anti-Judaism, hatred and persecution of Jews. In an effort to remedy this, the Jewish-Christian Dialogue symposium was formed in 1947 and continues today. Jewish and Christian leaders and ordinary congregation members of all ages get together regularly to get to know each other and to discuss scriptures or issues that are important to them. There are often guest speakers and then general discussion among the people at the meeting. Sometimes groups of Christians and Jews travel to Israel together, visiting sites that are important to their religions. Recently,

to bathe, she discovered the baby in the basket. She named him Moshe (known to Christians and others as Moses) and determined to take him home with her. Miriam offered to find a nurse, and the princess hired Jocheved for the task.

Raised and educated in the palace, Moses one day discovered who he really was – the son of slaves. It must have been shocking, but there were more shocks to come.

Murder, flight, marriage, and the shepherd's life occupied Moshe, until one day, God called him to lead his people out of Egypt and back into the Promised Land (Canaan). Moshe proved to be a reluctant hero. Only after hearing God's voice in a burning bush and seeing ten plagues attack the Egyptians did he lead the people away. For 3000 years now, Pesach has celebrated the story of how Moshe, his brother Aaron and sister Miriam led the Israelites across the Red Sea and into freedom. The book of Exodus (meaning "going out") tells how for 40 years the people wandered the desert, how God called Moshe up Mount Sinai and gave him the Ten Commandments, carved in stone, and how Moshe received the Torah. At last, within sight of the Promised Land, Moshe died. The people followed Joshua into the "land of milk and honey," and the pages of history turned.

In the centuries following, the people chose kings to rule them; God chose prophets to advise or scold the kings when they failed to rule with compassion and justice. The greatest king was the one who began as

some Christian churches have published documents that honestly look at their scriptures and find out which ones have caused problems and what can be done about them. One example of this is the United Church of Canada's document called *Bearing Faithful Witness*.

a Bethlehem shepherd around 1000 BCE. He killed the giant Goliath with a slingshot and became a respected warrior, great lover and enduring poet. His name was David.

David reigned as king into his old age and is celebrated as the one who established the rituals and traditions of religious worship. This means that when people had to endure hardship, for example, if they were invaded, exiled or their Temple destroyed, they were still able to worship God in a meaningful way.

Although Israel is geographically small, the land gives easy access to Africa, Europe, and Asia. Everyone, it seems, has wanted to control it. By 586 BCE, Jerusalem was a beautiful and sophisticated city; its crowning glory was the magnificent Temple,

built by King Solomon. But in that horrific year, the Babylonians invaded, conquered Jerusalem, destroyed the Temple, and exiled educated Jews to what is today called Iraq.

During Purim, Jews celebrate wise and beautiful Queen Esther. Around 500 BCE, she became Queen of Persia. (The king did not know that she was Jewish.) Haman, the king's prime minister hated Jews because they refused to bow down to him; they said they would only bow down to God. Enraged, Haman decided to kill them all and cast lots (purim) to decide a date. Esther heard of the plan. Taking her life in her hands, she sent word for her people to pray. Then she invited the king and Haman to dinner. She exposed Haman for the evil man he was. The gallows he'd built to kill Esther's

Yad Vashem

Yad Vashem (which translates as "a monument and a name") is the Holocaust Martyrs' and Heroes' Remembrance Authority in Jerusalem. There, visitors can go to museums to see artifacts and photographs from the ghettos, concentration and death camps. There is a children's memorial, where the names of some of the one-and-a-half-million children who died in the death camps are read aloud (not all of the names are known). There is an art gallery showing

cousin Mordecai became his own place of death.

Eventually, the exiled Jews returned home and, with the leader Ezra, began rebuilding the Temple around 515 BCE. Their lives began again. But this story was repeated again and again. Over time other superpowers invaded: from Persia (now Iran), Greece, and, in 63 BCE, the 300-year Roman occupation began. During this particular occupation, Jesus of Nazareth became a controversial teacher. Some of his followers believed him to be the Messiah. He was executed by the Romans around 33 CE. Some followers of Jesus eventually left the synagogue, joined with other non-Jewish followers and established the Christian church. Some of these people accused Jews of killing the son of God, and this idea was written into what became Christian scriptures. Even to this day, there are some Christians who believe this accusation. This has led to 2000 years of grief for Jews.

After the Romans destroyed the second Temple in 70 CE, most Jews dispersed to Africa and Europe. This changed how Jews worshipped. Although rabbis continued to teach and lead, the priesthood disappeared, meaning that the congregation began to take priestly responsibility. To this day, when ten adult Jews are present, a service of worship can be held. Services may be led by a rabbi, a cantor, or any adult member of the synagogue. In the 500s CE, the Talmud (writings of the rabbis) was collected and finalized.

For the next 1500 years, there were periods of peace and periods of violence, as various leaders wanted control

the drawings and pictures created by children, teens and adults as they lived the last days of their lives. There are gardens, sculptures, book stores and archives. There is also a garden and memorial dedicated to the "Righteous Among the Nations," which honours non-Jews, such as Oskar Schindler, who risked their lives to rescue Jews.

The Holocaust Memorial in Washington, DC, is another place to learn. The purpose of all the memorials, of International Holocaust Remembrance Day (which was declared by the United Nations in 2005 and which takes place on January 27) and of the day of religious observance Yom HaShoah is to help people remember and understand world history and to encourage everyone to work for justice, peace, and human rights.

of the area for religious, political, and economic reasons. In the late 600s, Jerusalem was under Muslim control. The Dome of the Rock, one of the most holy mosques for Muslims, was built on top of the site of the Temple in Jerusalem. The Christian Crusades followed. In the 1500s, the Muslim Ottoman Empire won control of the region. In 1918, World War I enabled the British to occupy the region. They kept control until after World War II ended.

In all these centuries, through all the forced changes, Jewish people held onto their traditions and kept the covenant that Avraham had made with God: "I will be your God and you will be my people." In some countries, during some times, Jews were free to practise their faith; in other times and countries, they were persecuted. In parts of Europe, they were forced to live in ghettos. In Russia, sword-bearing Cossacks swept through Jewish communities, raping, killing, and burning for no reason. In the early 1900s, many European Jews migrated to Israel and began creating farms in the desert and building a nation. In the 1930s, the Nazis gained power in Germany. This spelled catastrophe. Many Jews fled the hateful policies of the Nazi regime, but not enough of them.

During World War II, the Nazis systematically murdered six million European Jews, including one-and-a-half-million children. It is difficult to imagine that number of people being transported, starved, worked, and murdered. One of the most notorious death camps was at Auschwitz, in occupied Poland.

ANNE FRANK

In 1948, three years after the horror of the Holocaust, the United Nations voted to create the modern state of Israel. The world hoped that there, at last, Jews could live in safety and in peace. The United Nations arranged for one-third of the land in the area to be allotted for the state of Israel; Palestine would retain two thirds. This was not acceptable to everyone.

Five neighbouring countries attacked almost immediately. The first thing Israelis faced in their home country was going to war to defend it. Another war in 1967 resulted in Israel occupying more land than they had originally been allotted by the United Nations. This occupation is on-going, producing continuing unrest as well as outbursts of violence between political leaders of the Israelis, Palestinians, and some neighbouring Arab countries. Gaza is one of the world's oldest refugee camps; about one-million Palestinians live there today. The Palestinians also live in East Jerusalem and in an area called the West Bank.

Judaism teaches that there is one God, creator of the universe, and that if God's laws are followed, compassion, love, and justice will follow. Judaism also teaches that a Messiah will come to finally banish evil from the world. People have different understandings of "Messiah." Some believe it's an actual person, others understand it to be an era when everyone works together for a just and peaceful world.

Since ancient times, wherever Jews were exiled or chose to live, they established rich cultural and economic lives. Wherever they settle, they make far-reaching contributions to society, particularly in the areas of law, medicine, philosophy, music, the development of the film industry, theatre, psychiatry, and literature. These contributions continue to enrich our lives today, and the ancient stories – from the time of Avraham and Sarah – continue to echo through the lives of People of the Book today.

Rituals and Ceremonies

Rites of Passage

Brit Milah

On the eighth day after birth, male infants receive a Hebrew name and are circumcised. This act is a reminder of the ancient covenant God made with Avraham. This is a solemn religious ceremony, which is followed by a meal and celebration with family and friends. Female babies may receive a Hebrew name and a blessing.

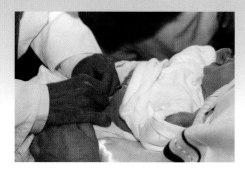

During early childhood, both boys and girls learn the stories, rituals and traditions of their faith. Around the time of the bar mitzvah or bat mitzvah ceremony, some families gather to tell stories about their relatives and ancestors that the initiate may not know.

Bar Mitzvah

After a boy turns 13, he celebrates becoming a "son of the commandment." (Bar means "son," and mitzvah means "commandment.") In this coming-of-age ceremony, he reads from the Torah and speaks to the congregation about the passage and its meaning. From then on, he has the rights and responsibilities of an adult in the congregation. There is often a great welcoming celebration for him after the ceremony.

Bat Mitzvah In modern times, after a girl turns 12, she celebrates her bat mitzvah. (Bat means "daughter.") She reads from the Torah and makes a presentation to the congregation about her understanding of the reading. After her family and friends celebrate, the daughter of the commandment can assume the responsibilities and rights of maturity. (This ceremony for girls does not exist in Orthodox Judaism.)

Golden Rule

What is hateful to you,

do not do to your neighbour.

~ HILLEL, TALMUD, SHABBAT 31A

Chapter 5

Buddhism

Green Rule

Cut down the forest of desire,

not the forest of trees.

~ DHAMMAPADA 283

Introducing: Nina Ha

My name is Nina Ha. I'm currently 17 years old, and in grade 12. Piano has been one of my favourite hobbies since I was eight. I am a volunteer at the Peter Lougheed Health Centre, and I enjoy being there every week.

Were you born into your religion or did you convert?

I was born and raised a Buddhist.

Briefly describe your home and family.

I live with my mom, older brother, younger sister and my grandma. We have a pet bunny, who has only been with us for almost two years. My siblings and I were born and raised in Calgary, Alberta.

For you, what would make a great weekend?

A great weekend would be spending time with both my family and friends, and no homework.

What worries or concerns you about the world or your life these days?

I'm sure there are lots of issues in the world today that many people are concerned about. The world is becoming more and more unfriendly these days. We all share Earth, and I don't see why everyone can't get along.

Where do you learn the stories and traditions in your religion?

I hear stories and learn about my religion during lectures at the temple. My mom has stories playing in the car and at home. When I was little, every night before bed my mom would read different stories about being compassionate and kind to animals.

In what ways do you think your religion helps you live your life?

Buddhism helps me in many ways. One, being at the temple relieves a lot of the stress I have from school and other things. The calm environment along with many friendly faces always brings a smile to my face. It's just so comforting to be in a place where everyone is singing, praying together, getting along and sharing stories.

Are there ways that your religion is a problem for you?

My religion has not yet been an issue since my friends are Buddhists too. I'm not sure how other people view Buddhism, but it doesn't really matter as long as I know I'm sincere with what I believe in.

Does your religion have anything special to say to teens or children?

When I was part of the Avatamsaka Monastery Youth Group, we focused a lot on getting along with others around us and returning as much as we can to the community. We went to the Mustard Seed (a Christian humanitarian organization that helps homeless people) a couple of times to help serve meals. That experience made me realize how grateful I am to have the things I have today.

What two or three things would you like people to know about your religion?

I want everyone to know Buddhism can be practised by anyone, anytime, and anywhere.

Have you ever been (or would you like to be) part of an interfaith event, worship or action?

I have never been part of an interfaith event. I would like to be part of one because I believe all religions pray for peace on Earth. Although different religions have different beliefs, world peace is probably what every religion wishes to see. And bringing different religions together is one big step to success.

People have talked often about what divides people who practise different religions. What do you think could bring (or is bringing) religious people together?

As mentioned above, I think that world peace is something all religions support.

What is your wish for the youth of the world?

I wish all youth in the world the opportunity to become educated so that they mature into great people who can make a big difference.

Buddha and Jesus

Some people make comparisons between Buddhism and Christianity. Buddha was born into a Hindu family. Jesus was born into a Jewish family. Both rebelled against the way the religious leadership of their day treated the poor and the way the leaders of their day misused their religious power. Both Buddha and Jesus have amazing and miraculous birth stories with spec-

Buddhist Prayer for Peace

*May all beings everywhere plagued
with sufferings of body and mind
quickly be freed from their illnesses.*

*May those frightened cease to be afraid,
and may those bound be free.*

*May the powerless find power,
and may people think of befriending
one another.*

*May those who find themselves in trackless,
fearful wilderness –
the children, the aged, the unprotected –
be guarded by beneficial celestials,
and may they swiftly attain Buddhahood.*

From: http://www.indianchild.com/hindu_prayers.htm

A Story of Buddhism

The beginning of Buddhism is woven with beautiful stories. King Suddhodana and, Hindus living in India, prayed for a child for years. Finally, with a revelation through a miraculous and sacred dream, the queen became pregnant. In 563 BCE, beneath the sal tree, Queen Maha-Maya gave birth to her son, a child so radiant that the world held its breath. Peace surrounded the planet, birds burst into song. They named him Siddhartha Gautama of the Shakyas.

Thumbnail Sketch

Who is the founder? Siddhartha Gautama, known as the Buddha.

When did it start? 600 BCE.

Are there any foundational sacred texts? Sutra (Buddha's teachings), Vinaya (Rules of Discipline) and Abhidharma (commentary).

In what places do people practise? In temples, monasteries, at shrines in homes, workplaces and on roadsides.

tacular supernatural events and even the cosmos celebrating their births. Both became leaders who wandered the countryside with their disciples, teaching, confronting, encouraging and breaking the rules of the day. (The differ-

ences are striking, too. Jesus was killed after three years of teaching. The Buddha lived to 80.) Today, the followers of both Jesus and of Buddha live everywhere in the world and the cultures of different countries add flavour to these

very old religions.

For people interested in comparative religions (the study of two or more religions), Christianity and Buddhism have lots to offer. The books *Living Buddha, Living Christ* by Thich Nhat Hanh and *The Good*

Heart: A Buddhist Perspective on the Teachings of Jesus by His Holiness The Dalai Lama are two examples of this exploration.

The king wanted only the very best for his son. Besides the best clothes, food and care that money could provide, he also called for soothsayers to learn how to best protect his son. The story tells us that a wise man said that if the boy could be kept from seeing the sorrows of the world, then he would grow up to become a great king. Otherwise, he would lead a religious life. The father did his best to keep the sorrows of the world from his son's sight. The boy grew up, married, and had a son. But in all the luxury of the palace, he felt restless. One fateful night, he left the palace and went out to see the city. And there he saw four things that changed his life: an old man, a diseased man, a dead man, and a monk. Siddhartha had come across suffering for the first time in his life. He wanted to learn more. He wanted to find out how to eliminate suffering from the world. This desire led him to leave his family, his luxury, and to give up everything. He cut off his hair,

What are spiritual leaders are called? Lamas, monks, nuns, Rinpoches, thay, sensai.

Where is the tradition practised? Mainly in Asia and the Far East; around the world.

What are the main branches of the tradition? Mahayana, which is mainly practised in Tibet and China; and Theravada, which is practised in Viet Nam, Myanmar, Ceylon and Thailand. Zen (begun in

Japan) and Vajrayana (begun in Tibet) are forms of Mahayana Buddhism.

Are there special holy days? Spring and fall equinox; Wesak Day (which happens at the full moon of the fourth month between May and June) celebrates the birth, enlightenment, and entry into Nirvana

of the Buddha; Vassa is rainy season retreat; and Kathina is when monks and nuns are offered robes, food or monastic necessities. The Buddhist calendar is lunar.

The Three Baskets of Wisdom

The following items are the foundational sacred texts for Buddhism.

1) Sutra Pitaka (the Teaching Basket) – Records of the actual experiences of Buddha.

2) Vinaya Pitaka (the Discipline Basket) – A rule book for monks and nuns.

3) Abhidharma Pitaka (the Higher Doctrine Basket) – An explanation on the teachings of Buddha. Most of these are called sutras.

put on a monk's robe, and joined the Hindu holy people in the forest.

He lived with them for years of study, meditation, and deprivation. He was so enthusiastic about this life that he almost starved himself to death. In the end, he decided that neither a life of luxury nor a life of deprivation were good. He chose the middle way. After six more years of thinking, Siddhartha sat under a Bo tree to meditate. There, he repeatedly felt tempted to give up his quest, but he did not. Just as dawn was breaking, Siddhartha's mind opened to the mystery he longed to solve. For 48 more days, he sat beneath the tree, blissfully preparing his mind and heart for the work ahead.

From a life of luxury to a life of poverty and hunger, Siddhartha now turned to his life's work. For 45 years, he walked throughout the land, teaching, establishing monasteries, giving counsel and advice, and showing by example that returning to the sacred source every day, through meditation, is essential.

Like other charismatic spiritual leaders, Sid-

Words to Know

Buddha: one who has developed all positive qualities and eliminated all negative qualities. An enlightened being; one who is "awake."

Dharma: the practice of the truth; the Buddha's teachings.

Karma: the law of cause and effect.

Mala: prayer beads. Many Buddhists wear these wrapped around their wrists.

Mandalas: are symbols of the universe. (They can also represent the palaces of different Buddhas.) Mandalas are sometimes made with coloured sand; when complete, they are swept into a urn then offered to rivers or lakes as purification and blessing with ritual prayers. This action reminds people that nothing is permanent.

Three Refuges: Buddha, dharma and sangha; these make up the basic orientation for Buddhist life

Mantra: a short chant (usually the name of a Buddha) recited over and over to clear, protect and purify the mind and gain spiritual realizations.

The Three Poisons

Greed   Hate   Ignorance

dhartha was asked who or what he was. His famous answer was, "I am awake." The translation of this answer is how the word Buddhism came to be. Budh is a Sanskrit root word meaning "to know" or "to wake up." In his 80th year, the Buddha died peacefully, leaving his teaching and a tradition that went on to spread around the world.

One characteristic of Buddhism is that most Buddhists do not mind joining in other people's religious ceremonies. The Buddha taught not to commit any unwholesome actions, but to accumulate virtuous deeds, to tame and train your own mind. This means abstaining from ten non-virtuous actions of body (killing, stealing, sexual misconduct), speech (lying, causing dissention, harmful words, idle chatter), and mind (ill will, greediness). Being compassionate is more important than what people say they believe. Dharma is more a way of life than religion. It can be followed by anyone without converting to the faith. Buddha did not want anyone to worship him, but to experience his teaching, realize the truth, and

Nirvana: a state of peace.

Precept: guideline. There are five basic precepts for following dharma.

Rinpoche: a Tibetan Buddhist title of honour for a spiritual leader.

Samsara: rounds of rebirths that never free one from suffering.

Sangha: virtuous community.

Sensai: a Japanese term that means "teacher"; a name for a spiritual leader.

Thay: a Vietnamese term that means "teacher"; a name for a spiritual leader.

Wheel of Life: represents Buddha's teaching. It shows six realms of samsara, caused by desire, hatred and ignorance, and the twelve links representing freedom. A painting of the Wheel of Life was given by Buddha to royalty. When the king studied the picture, he attained wisdom.

Zen Buddhism: a branch of Mahayana Buddhism that focuses on meditation.

The Three Universal Truths

1. **Everything Changes.** There is only one thing for sure in life: everything changes. People are born, grow up, grow old and die. Plants, rocks, everything is in a constant state of change. Our ideas about life also change. People once believed that the world was flat, but now we know that it is round.

2. **Nothing is lost in the universe.** Everyone and everything is interconnected. We depend on and react to one another constantly. If we destroy something around us, we destroy ourselves. If we cheat another, we cheat ourselves. Understanding this truth, the Buddha and his disciples never killed any animal.

3. **The law of cause and effect rules.** Our thoughts and actions determine the kind of life we can have. No one can avoid *dukkha* ("disappointment and suffering"). But

become a Buddha themselves. He said his teaching was like a raft to be used to cross the river of *samsara* (which means "suffering"). Only a fool will carry the raft on his back and walk up and down the riverbank without using the opportunity to cross the river.

Another distinguishing characteristic of Buddhism is that there is no creator God. Since the first Buddha, there have also been other men – and women too – who have attained enlightenment and become Buddhas. The Buddha taught that both men and women can attain enlightenment. The Tibetan titles Lama and Rinpoche are used for both male and female masters.

In the Buddha's time, and even now in some religions, this acknowledgement of women was a controversial idea, because so many people believe that only men should be religious leaders.

There are many versions of the Buddha shown in statues and paintings, but Buddhists do not worship these statues.

Buddhists pay respect to the Buddha's statues and teachings by bowing low, lighting incense, and walking round and round to purify negative karma.

About 200 years after the death of the Buddha, Emperor Asoka of the Magadhan Empire was busy expanding his empire. One story is told that there were Buddhists among his subjects and that he was mildly interested in what they had to say. After a particularly gruesome campaign on the battlefield, he went home to seriously explore this peaceful way of life. Eventually he con-

every moment we create new karma by what we say, do and think. Karma teaches us to create a good future. The Buddha said, "If you carefully plant a good seed, you will joyfully gather good fruit."

verted to Buddhism and encouraged his subjects to do the same. Buddhism became the state religion and he even banned hunting. He was so enthusiastic about his new religion, in fact, that he sent his son Mahinda to Sri Lanka to tell the king about it. Sri Lanka, too, adopted Buddhism as the state religion, and so the new movement spread.

The teachings of the Buddha were memorized and passed down orally for about 400 years. Around 100 BCE, the followers gathered in Sri Lanka and decided it was time to write the teachings. And so they began writing on palm leaves and eventually filled three baskets. The Buddha's teachings are called *Tipitaka*, meaning "three baskets," because of this fact. It was around this time that philosophical differences came up. People separated into two different streams of Buddhism: *Mahayana* (meaning "Large Vehicle," which includes Tibetan, Japanese and Chinese Buddhism) and *Theravada* (meaning "The Teaching of the Elders," which is practised mainly in southeast Asia). Mahayana developed distinctive characteristics and rituals, such as chanting and prayer wheels. Devotees follow reincarnated lamas.

From 100 CE until the Communist era (mid 1900s), Buddhism flourished in China, along with Taoism and Confucianism. Since then, religions have been discouraged in China and there have been periods of great oppression and persecution. In the 1950s, many monasteries were destroyed both in China and Tibet.

The Four Noble Truths

1. Suffering and disappointment are part of life.

2. Disappointment occurs because we crave things or are ignorant.

3. We can enjoy life although it isn't perfect.

4. By following the Noble Eightfold Path, we can gain wisdom for living a fulfilling life.

Buddhism spread to Korea by 400 CE. In the sixth century, Buddhist temples were appearing in Burma, Vietnam, Laos, Cambodia, and Japan. Buddhism became the state religion in Japan. In the 12th century, Zen Buddhism was developed, which is practised today worldwide. The movement remained strong there until the 1850s, when the cult of the emperor emerged (the emperor was seen as a deity).

Buddhism travelled to Tibet around 800 CE, taken there by an Indian master who, it is said, chased all the demons from the country! The movement thrived in Tibet under the leadership of successive Dalai Lamas, who serve as spiritual leaders and advisors. In 1959, the Chinese government invaded Tibet. The Dalai Lama and thousands of others were forced to flee. They live in exile still, in the town of Dharamsala, India. Dharamsala has become a centre for Buddhists and for others from around the world who want to learn about Buddhism and receive teachings from the Dalai Lama. The Dalai Lama travels around the world speaking about peace, Buddhism, and freedom for his native land. He is a recipient of the Nobel Peace Prize and many other honours for his message of peace in the world. He is particularly interested in speaking with young people.

In September 2006, he joined 11 other Nobel Peace Prize laureates at the University of Denver in Colorado, at PeaceJam. (The other laureates were Shirin Ebadi, Rigoberta MenchuTum, Mairead Corrigan Maguire, Jody Williams, Wangari Maathai, Betty

The Five Precepts

1. Practise loving kindness to all creatures; do not kill.

2. Practise generosity; do not steal.

3. Abstain from sexual misconduct and sensual overindulgence.

4. Practise honesty with yourself and others; do not lie.

5. Keep your mind clear; do not abuse yourself with drugs or alcohol.

Williams, Archbishop Desmond Tutu, Joseph Rotblat, Adolfo Perez Esquivel, Bishop Carlos Belo, and Oscar Arias.)

Peace Jam is an international education program to bring youth and Nobel Laureates together to inspire a new generation of peacemakers who want to transform themselves, their communities, and the world. (www.peacejam.org)

On June 22, 2006, the Canadian Parliament voted unanimously to offer His Holiness the Dalai Lama Canadian citizenship. This honour was meant to show how much Canadians value the Dalai Lama's work for peace and non-violence in the world. This unusual honour has only been granted to two other people in the world – Nelson Mandela, Nobel Peace Prize laureate and the first black prime minister of South Africa; and Raouel Wallenberg of Hungary, who saved the lives of Jews during World War II.

Although Buddhism has been practised in North America by small groups since the 1850s, it became more visible in the 1960s, particularly Zen Buddhism and Tibetan Buddhism. This was partly because in the 1960s young people were turning on to peace and looking for ways to achieve it both politically and spiritually. When stars like Yoko Ono and John Lennon of the Beatles explored Buddhism, it became an interesting path to millions of others. Today, Buddhist temples are seen in many Western cities and Buddhists are very active in peace and interfaith organizations. Popular writers such as Thich Nhat Hanh, a Vietnamese monk, have also helped to make the practice of Buddhism accessible to everyone.

The Noble Eightfold Path

1. Right understanding and viewpoint (based on the Four Noble Truths).

2. Right values and attitude (be compassionate rather than selfish).

3. Right speech (don't tell lies; avoid harsh, abusive speech and avoid gossip).

4. Right action (help others, live honestly, don't harm living things and take care of the environment).

5. Right work (do something useful and avoid jobs that harm others).

6. Right effort (encourage good, helpful thoughts and discourage unwholesome destructive thoughts).

7. Right mindfulness (be aware of what you feel, think, and do).

8. Right concentration (practise calming your mind and meditation, which leads to nirvana).

Rites of Passage

In some communities, a boy entering puberty may spend a few weeks in a monastery as a sign of entering into maturity and growing into responsibility. He may be dressed like a young prince then have his head shaved and be dressed in monastic robes. This ritual is to remember and imitate Buddha in his early years. The boy will spend weeks studying scriptures and writings with monks, usually at the beginning of the rainy season at the celebration of Vassa. A similar ceremony is possible for girls who choose to become nuns.

Meditation

People take up meditation in many different religious or spiritual traditions and for many different reasons. Learning from one another about various techniques can be helpful and interesting. Some may take up meditation as a spiritual discipline or a method of self-discovery. Others may do it to relieve stress and to take time out from a busy life. Some do it to honour the sacred, to explore a thought or piece of sacred writing. A medical doctor might recommend meditation as a way to lower blood pressure. A counsellor might suggest it as a way to lessen emotional upheaval.

Birth and Enlightenment under a Tree

Shortly before Queen Maha-Maya was to give birth to her first child, she followed the custom of the time and set out on a journey to visit her mother and father. En route, she stopped at a grove of sal trees. When the queen reached out her hand to touch the beautiful tree, the tree bent down toward her. Immediately, she realized that the time had come for her deliver. She directed her servants to place a screen around her. Standing beneath the tree and holding a branch for support, she brought her son into the world. It is said that as soon as Buddha was born, he took seven steps. From each step, a lotus flower sprouted. He said, "I am the guide for this world."

Thirty-five years later, Gautama had married, become a father and spent six years in study, meditation, travel and deprivation. One full-moon night, he sat meditating beneath a bo tree. He believed that he was close to reaching understanding. Here he sat, while the temptation to give up challenged him. But understanding and the dawn broke.

This Great Awakening transformed a man into a Buddha. It is said that lotuses bloomed on every tree and that all earth rejoiced.

Lost in rapture, the Buddha remained beneath the tree for a week.

An art teacher might suggest it to enhance creativity. People also meditate to seek enlightenment, as the Buddha did under the bo tree long ago.

The basic idea behind meditation is to still the mind. Most of us have about a million little memories, lists, thoughts, unfinished essays, new ideas or worries tugging at our minds all the time. Even if we turn off the television, computer, iPod, Blackberry and cell phone, we are left with a mind filled with chatter. It can be hard to get to know us with all that confusing noise going on.

Once we have cleared away some of the external noise, we need to find a quiet place where we will not be disturbed. This can be in a chapel or temple, by a river or in our own bedroom. Because our minds are so active, it helps to have something to help us quiet our minds and focus. People use various items such as a candle flame, a calming or holy picture, a plant or blade of grass. Some use meditative music. Many people use a simple, repetitive chant or mantra, singing or

Prayer Flags

Colourful prayer flags are hung between trees or poles, on verandas or anywhere in Tibet, India and many other places. These cotton red, green, white and yellow flags are printed with prayers. They are meant to wave in the wind, sending compassion and peace far and wide until they disintegrate.

saying the words over and over again as a means of finding quiet.

Breathing is extremely important in meditation. Focused deep breathing is helpful whenever we are entering into stressful situations such as writing an exam, taking a driving test or speaking in public. Even though we all know how to breathe to stay alive, meditation and yoga teachers help us to become aware of how we breathe. When our breaths are shallow and quick, it can trigger our bodies to become anxious and alert, ready for danger. Learning to breathe by focusing on our whole bodies can help us become calm, relaxed and awake. People who smoke cigarettes and inhale the smoke are imitating deep breathing in an unhealthy, toxic way. People who learn to meditate will learn deep breathing in a way that will enhance their lives.

Golden Rule

Treat not others in ways that you yourself would find hurtful.

~ UDANA-VARGA 5.18

Chapter 6

Christianity

Green Rule

The kingdom of God is like a mustard seed that someone sowed in the garden; it grew and became a tree, and the birds of the air made their nests in its branches.

~ LUKE 13:18 (NEW TESTAMENT))

Introducing: Ryan Workman

My name is Ryan Workman. I am 15, in grade 11. I have a number of hobbies, including sketching, writing, reading and dramatic role-playing. I would say that I am passionate about the world environmental situation; it greatly concerns me. I also feel that there needs to be a drastic change in our world community in relation to attitudes and actions for dealing with war, poverty, disease and the many other preventable problems of the world. I have participated actively in many peace and environmental movements, such as Make Poverty History (a campaign to end world poverty) and the David Suzuki Foundation.

Were you born into your religion or did you convert?
I have only ever attended the United Church of Canada.

Briefly describe your home and family.
I was born in North Bay, Ontario, but have moved several times since and now live in Calgary, Alberta. I have two brothers, who are 12 and nine. I also have two parents.

For you, what would make a great weekend?
For me, a great weekend would include playing the computer, some tennis with my brother or doing lots of reading. It could also include doing some sketching or writing, and maybe doing something with my family (such as having a late-night board game, going to the Calgary Stampede or attending a music festival).

What worries or concerns you about the world or your life these days?
I have many concerns about the world these days. Global warming is a very scary thing; most sources that I've seen suggest that it will have devastating repercussions within the next ten to 20 years. Already it is having a very negative impact. I can see changes in Calgary's weather, and I feel global warming is responsible. Over the last few years, hail is becoming a frequent weather phenomenon; just a short while ago, a storm rained hail the size of my fist on southern Alberta. I worry about our world's political environment, filled with war and the possibility of the usage of nuclear weapons. In my life, I have concerns also, but who doesn't? The greater concerns for the world are part of my life - trying to figure out how I can help prevent them. I must do my schoolwork, work through difficulties with family and friends, etc.

Where do you learn the stories and traditions in your religion?

I learned specifically about stories and legends of Christianity in several places: in my Sunday-school class, at Awana Christian camp, and at Future Quest, a theological youth camp. I have also spent most of my life completely immersed in a solely Christian environment; for example, in movies I watched, when they referred to going to church, this would mean a Christian church.

In what ways do you think your religion helps you live your life?

Religion, for me, is more a way to figure out values. I don't find it as important to know the stories and the theology as I find it to know what my values are. This I can explore through discussion with people interested in their own theology, such as the people at church.

Are there ways that your religion is a problem for you?

There are no ways that I find my religion to be a problem for me.

Does your religion have anything special to say to teens or children?

One of the values of the United Church is supporting children and youth. There has been a bit of discussion of hypocrisy within the church about the subject, such as saying this but putting the teen youth group away from the main congregation because we are noisy. There is a teen youth group that I attend, and I get to have a community of other youth to talk things through.

Have you ever been (or would you like to be) part of an interfaith event, worship or action?

I have been part of an interfaith discussion on how to assist Muslims in Canada deal with the potential (and likely) backlash against them after suspected terrorists were arrested in Ontario.

People have talked often about what divides people who practise different religions. What do you think could bring (or is bringing) religious people together?

What could bring religions together is that they all are, at the very basic level, the same, asking for people to respect their fellow human beings. Only the customs and ceremonies required are different.

What is your wish for the youth of the world?

For the youth of the world, I want us to be able to correct the mistakes that our predecessors have made, to follow a different path. I also wish for us, as for all people, to be able to live in peace.

Do you have any advice for religious or other leaders in the world today?

I would advise all leaders who have control over nuclear weapons, especially the United States, to disarm them. I would suggest that they all look for ways to work towards a clean environment. I would say they should look for peaceful means of working through their differences.

What two or three things would you like people to know about your religion?

What are some things I would like you to know about the United Church? It is very open, at least our church is. You are not required to believe in a certain set of rules.

The Lord's Prayer

In Jerusalem, there is a beautiful courtyard attached to the 12th-century *Pater Noster* (which translates as "Our Father") Church. In the courtyard, the Lord's Prayer is written in 110 languages. When you visit, you see people from all over the world standing in front of and saying the prayer written in their language. The prayer is found in Matthew and Luke's gospels in the Bible.

Jesus said, when you pray, say:

Father, hallowed be your name,

your kingdom come.

Your will be done,

on Earth as it is in Heaven.

Give us each day our daily bread.

Forgive us our sins, for we also forgive

everyone who sins against us.

And lead us not into temptation.

Deliver us from evil.

Some versions add:

For yours is the kingdom, the power,

and the glory,

For ever and ever,

Amen.

A Story of Christianity

Every December, Christians tell the story of Mary, a 14-year-old Jewish girl living in the town of Nazareth. Like the whole region, Nazareth was under military occupation, which meant that Mary was accustomed to checkpoints and seeing Roman soldiers everywhere. She had been planning to marry a local carpenter named Joseph. It wasn't hard for her to imagine her future: like all good Jewish wives, she would

Thumbnail Sketch

Who are the founders? The followers of Jesus Christ, especially Paul of Tarsus.

When did it start? About 2000 years ago.

Are there any foundational sacred texts? The Bible, which consists of 66 books. The first 39 are called the Hebrew Bible, Hebrew scriptures or Tanakh; the remaining books, written after the birth of Jesus, are referred to as the New or Christian Testament.

The Magnificat or Song of Mary

Mary said:
My soul glorifies the Lord, and my spirit rejoices in God my Saviour, for God has remembered the humble, servant state.

From now on, generations will call me blessed because of the wonderful things God has done. Holy is God's name.

God's mercy extends to those who offer respect, from generation to generation. God has performed mighty deeds and scattered those who are proud in their inmost thoughts.

God has brought down rulers from their thrones but has lifted up the humble.

God has filled the hungry with good things but has sent the rich away empty.

God has helped servant Israel, and remembered to be merciful to Abraham and his descendants forever, just as was promised our ancestors.

~ adapted from Luke 1:46–55 (New Testament)

stay out of trouble, marry young, have children, cook, clean, garden, spin, sew, keep the Sabbath and then watch her grandchildren arrive. But Mary's life turned upside down when an angel appeared to her and announced that she was pregnant.

The story of the birth of her son, Jesus, is a story filled with danger and great love. It is also a story of great hope. One famous passage in the Bible is Mary's Magnificat, a song and a prophecy that God will side with the poor and the powerful will be brought down.

Mary's fiancé, Joseph, is instructed by an angel to care for Mary and not abandon her because the child she is carrying is the child of God. When Mary is almost ready to give birth, Joseph is forced to go to Bethlehem to register for a government census. The two make the journey only to find

In what places do people worship? Mainly in churches or cathedrals.

What are worship leaders called? Ministers, pastors (Protestant) or priests (Eastern Orthodox and Roman Catholic).

Where is the tradition practised? Worldwide.

What are the main branches of the tradition? Roman Catholic, Protestant and Eastern Orthodox.

Are there special holy days? Sundays; Christmas is the traditional day to celebrate the birth of Jesus; Advent is the month leading up to Christmas; Lent consists of 40 days of reflection and repentance leading up to Easter; Good Friday (or God's Friday) commemorates the day that Jesus was executed; Easter celebrates the day that Jesus was seen by his friends, three days after he was killed (this miracle is called the Resurrection); the term also refers to the Easter "season," which lasts 50 days. Christians celebrate Jesus' resurrection (Easter) on the Sunday following the first full moon after spring solstice. Like Easter, the term Pentecost refers both to a specific day (which celebrates the birth of the church) and to an entire "season" of the church year.

The Celebration of the Last Supper

The celebration of the Last Supper (also called communion) is an important ritual in Christian churches. It re-enacts the final moments that Jesus had with his disciples before he was arrested and crucified. Like most Jews, they had gone to Jerusalem to celebrate the Passover (a festival recognizing the Israelites' freedom from slavery). After the meal ended, Jesus gave his friends something to remember him by. First, he washed their feet, as a servant would. Then he blessed the bread and wine and asked that his friends remember him. The parts and words vary in different denominations, but the ritual might begin with the leader holding bread and wine saying:

Leader: On the night before his death, Jesus took bread and thanked God, as we have thanked God. He broke the bread and gave it to his friends saying:

All: Take this, all of you, and eat it. And as you eat it, remember my body, broken for you.

that there is no room for them in an inn, and they must take shelter in a barn. The birth of Jesus is witnessed by Joseph, farm animals, and angels. As the story unfolds, the baby is visited by lowly shepherds and by great and wise kings. His life is then threatened by King Herod who, fearing that this king will take his power, orders that all baby boys in Bethlehem should be killed. Mary and Joseph flee to Egypt and stay until the old king dies and they can return to Nazareth.

It could be argued that Jesus didn't plan to plant the seeds for a whole new religion. He was a practising Jew, born into a wild and turbulent time in the history of the Middle East. His people had been living under the Roman military occupation for about 40 years, when he was born. The Jewish people were forced to pay high taxes to Caesar in far-away Rome and were treated like slaves in their own country. It was not unusual in those days for Rome to "teach a lesson," if the Jews complained about their lives or were suspected of planning an uprising: the Romans favoured crucifixion as a way to set an example and to keep the population quiet.

Tradition says that when Jesus was 30, God called him. He was baptized by his cousin John, called the Baptist, and then retreated to the desert where he faced demons that tempted him

Leader: After the meal had ended, he took the wine and thanked God for it. He passed the cup to his friends saying:

All: This is the cup of the new covenant God has made with you. Each time you drink from it, remember me.

Some churches perform this ritual every day or every Sunday. Others perform it monthly or a few times a year.

to follow other paths. In the end, he decided to take what he believed was God's path.

For three years, Jesus walked throughout the land teaching about a new vision for the people of God. His teachings were mostly through parables (a type of story) for he was a great storyteller. He was also known as a healer and miracle worker. He challenged injustices that he saw: he spoke publicly with women (who, at that time, were considered second-class citizens) and he touched people who were despised, such as lepers. He also challenged the authorities of the day. By the end of three years, he was popular and loved by many; he was

Words to Know

Communion: a sacred ritual of drinking wine or juice and eating bread (also called Eucharist, Mass or the Lord's Supper). It is the act of "being one" with God and one another. This ritual began at the last meal that Jesus and his friends shared.

Crucifix: a simple cross (at the time of Jesus) or (today) a cross with the figure of Jesus on it. The latter are seen in Catholic and Orthodox churches. (In Protestant churches, the cross is left empty, signifying that Jesus conquered death.)

Crucifixion: death on a cross. It was a common form of execution by the Romans.

Denomination: a religious group that has separated from the "parent" group. Within the three main branches of Christianity (Eastern Orthodox, Roman Catholic and Protestant) there are many denominations. Baptists, Presbyterians, Salvation Army, Episcopalians and Lutherans are examples of different denominations.

Ecumenism: The quest to bring together the various Christian denominations for dialogue, understanding and action.

Gospel, the: the message of Jesus about the kingdom of God; "the Gospels" refers to the four accounts of Jesus' life found in the part of the Bible known as the New Testament: The Gospel of Matthew, The Gospel of Mark, The Gospel of Luke, and the Gospel of John.

Ministry: service to the church.

Parable: a story containing an important teaching. Many rabbis at the time of Jesus used parables when teaching. Famous parables of Jesus can be found in the books of Matthew and Luke in the New Testament.

Reformation: movements of reform in the early 16th century. These affected every area of European life, including women's rights, education, medicine, church power, health, science and the arts.

Resurrection: to arise; to live again after death.

Sacraments: sacred Christian rituals such as baptism and communion. (Protestants and Catholics have different ideas about how many sacraments should be recognized.)

Christian Non-violence: the Work of Reverend Dr. Martin Luther King. Jr.

The third Monday of January is Martin Luther King Day, which was created to honour a man who helped to change the world. Martin Luther King, Jr. was born January 15, 1929, in Atlanta, Georgia. Like his father and grandfather, he became a Baptist (Protestant) minister. He said that his non-violent ideas and courage came from reading the American philosopher Henry Thoreau, learning about the Hindu activist Mahatma Gandhi of India (see Chapter 3) and believing the teachings of Jesus.

Dr. King believed that everyone should be treated with respect, but, as an African-American, he had learned early that segregation (separating racial groups) made this impossible. For example, even though he had played with a white friend in childhood, at age six, he and his friend were forced to go to separate schools and forbidden to play together.

At college, Dr. King read about civil disobedience in the writings of Henry David Thoreau. Thoreau wrote that if people would disobey unjust laws and follow their conscience, they could change the world. Dr. King also read about Mahatma Gandhi's struggle to free India from British rule by leading a peaceful revolution. After college, Dr. King married Coretta Scott and became a pastor in Montgomery, Alabama. Together

also ignored, feared, and hated. The Romans were afraid that he was stirring up a plot to fight them. Religious leaders feared that all the Jews would be punished if there was trouble; they thought Jesus was encouraging people to break Jewish laws. Eventually, the enemies of Jesus, helped by one of Jesus own friends, decided to get rid of him. After sharing the Passover meal (his Last Supper) with his friends, Jesus was arrested. The next day, Pontius Pilot, the Roman Emperor's local authority, sentenced Jesus to death by crucifixion.

Three days after his death, women friends discovered that the cave where Jesus had been buried was empty. For 40 days after, various friends saw him in different places: by the lake, on a road, in a meeting room. This miracle is called the Resurrection.

they helped shape a new plan for justice. When Rosa Parks boarded a bus on December 1, 1955, in Montgomery and refused to give up her seat to a white man, the plan was set in motion.

Dr. King and other African-Americans encouraged people to boycott Montgomery buses until all passengers had the same rights. People rode bicycles, walked, hitched rides, shared cars – some even rode mules – for more than one year. Bus companies lost a fortune. The mood turned ugly. Dr. King's home was firebombed; he and other leaders were threatened. People were jailed. Facing an angry mob, Dr. King said, "We must learn to meet hatred with love."

On November 13, 1956, the Supreme Court declared Alabama's bus segregation laws illegal. People in the United States and around the world knew again that non-violence is powerful. To celebrate, Dr. King and Reverend Glen Smiley, a white Christian, shared the front seat of a bus.

In his "Letter from Birmingham Jail," Dr. King wrote, "We will have to repent in this generation not merely for the hateful words and actions of the bad people but for the appalling silence of the good people." Dr. King was awarded the Nobel Peace Prize in 1964. He was the youngest man to receive it. After the death of Dr. King, the King Center in Atlanta, Georgia, was established to be a force in the world for creative, non-violent social change.

Jesus' friends believed that Jesus had risen from death and that he was the Messiah, the one promised by God. Some believed that he would bring justice at last and end the Roman occupation. Although it was still dangerous, these friends continued to tell the stories, heal and preach as Jesus had done. After about 60 years, the parables and stories of the life of Jesus were written down and collected together in the books called Matthew, Mark, Luke and John: the first four books of the New Testament. The Bible that Christians use is made up of the Jewish holy writings (which Jesus learned, read and preached) and a newer testament containing the stories of Jesus, the history of the early church, letters from the missionary Paul and a book called Revelation, which a disciple wrote vividly describing his visions from prison.

Paul of Tarsus, a Jewish Roman citizen, persecuted members of this new movement until he had a vision of Jesus. Afterward, he became a great missionary for the movement. The Christian Bible is full of his writings. For years, he travelled vast distances around the Mediterranean until he too was killed by Roman order. Three hun-

Women in Christianity

Women have always fulfilled various roles in Christianity. Women were among the early disciples of Jesus and helped continue the movement after his death. Although there are ancient writings about the leadership of women during the early days of the church, for centuries, men took on the role of priest, administrator and law maker. Despite notable exceptions, like the artist, writer, medicine woman, and mystic

dred years later, Christianity became the official religion of the Roman Empire.

The last 2000 years of Middle East and European history have been influenced by Christianity, and Christianity has been influenced by politics. Since the beginning, Christians believed that they were to "spread the Gospel," which means to go out and tell people the good news of Jesus and convert people from other faiths. They believed that if they didn't do this, they would burn in hell – and so would the non Christians. There have been millions of missionaries since Paul. Within about a thousand years after the death of Jesus, Christians could be found almost everywhere. The Eastern Orthodox branch of the church split from the Western Catholic tradition at this time having argued about the "correct" way to follow Jesus. Eastern Orthodox followers live mainly in what are now Russia, Ukraine, Serbia and Greece. In Europe, Christian ideas got tangled up with the politics of the day. The church was used to establish male dominance, and, around this time, Pope Urban II (the leader of the church based in Rome) urged men to join the Crusades and to make the land where Jesus had lived into a Christian place. The result was 300 years of war against Muslims and Jews.

Just about the time that Christopher Columbus sailed to the Americas in 1492, Europe turned upside down. Protesters tried to reform what they perceived as corrupt rule, both of kings and of the pope. This Reformation resulted in many changes in Europe, including the establishment of the Protestant Church. The Protestant reformers included John Hus in Bohemia, John Calvin in Switzerland, John Knox in Scotland and Martin Luther in Germany. All of them believed that the church had drifted away from the central

Hildegard of Bingen (who lived in the Middle Ages), the church mostly consisted of a hierarchy of men.

Today, Protestant women serve as priests and ministers and are free to lead national and international church bodies. Orthodox and Roman Catholic priests are still men.

teachings of the Bible. Some reformers left the Roman Catholic Church; others were thrown out of it. Originally written in Hebrew, then Greek, the Bible had been translated and copied into Latin by monks. In 1450, Johannes Gutenberg of Germany invented the

printing press and printed the first book, a Latin Bible. Around this time, the Bible began to appear in the languages of the people. At last, ordinary people who could read had access to the stories themselves.

Also around this time, European explorers who were looking for a trade route to China bumped into North America and decided that they had discovered it. They claimed the land for their king (of England, France, Portugal or Spain) and began the move-

ment of traders, farmers, fishers, and businessmen to and from this place. They also brought missionaries with them, although this spreading of the Gospel proved to be devastating to the spirituality and, in many cases, the lives of First Nations peoples, as the church today has learned.

Martin Luther

Over the next 500 years, Christianity continued to spread and to change. Every now and again, a new movement began, and a new denomination branched off from the main one. Today, there is an incredible range of denominations. Some are relatively small like the Quakers, known for their strong peace work; others are worldwide, like the Anglican Church (which is also called the Episcopal Church or the Church of England).

But there have also been many movements that bring Christians together. One of these is the Canadian Council of Churches, started in 1944

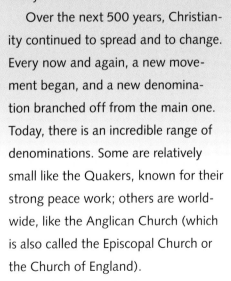

Quakers: Working for Peace on Earth and with Earth

The Religious Society of Friends, also known as the Quakers, began in 17th century England as a reform movement. It soon spread to other parts of the world and was influential in the United States. The Quakers played an important role in the anti-slavery movement, working for equality between men and women, and working for peace and non-violence. On both sides of the Atlantic, they have also been strong advocates for the human treatment of mentally ill people and prisoners.

One famous Quaker was Elizabeth Fry, who was born in 1780 in England. Her maiden name was Gurney. Although married and the mother of 11 children, Elizabeth worked hard for women who were in conflict with the law. This was

with its headquarters in Toronto, Ontario. This organization started organizations such as Project Ploughshares, which does peace research and education.

After the First World War, some European Christians began dreaming about an international organization to bring Christians together to work for common goals (even if they didn't agree on every detail about how to interpret the Bible or worship God.) Finally, after World War II, the dream was realized. The first meeting of the World Council of Churches took place in 1948 in Amsterdam, Holland. There were mostly men present because, in those days, mostly men were religious leaders. (Reverend Dr. Lois Wilson, of Toronto, became the first woman president in 1983.) The organization began with 147 Protestant and Eastern Orthodox representatives from 44 countries. Roman Catholics still have not joined, but representatives come to the assemblies and participate. Today, there are 342 participating churches from 120 countries.

The World Council of Churches, with headquarters in Geneva, Switzerland, has global programs that relate to five themes: faith and order; mission and ecumenical formation; justice, peace and creation; international affairs, peace and human security; and solidarity. The Youth Desk at the Council deals with issues such as climate change, HIV/AIDS, Christian-Muslim peace building, ecumenism and globalization. The Council employs interns from ages 18 to 30 in the Geneva office.

The Council declared 2001 to 2010 the Decade to Overcome Violence. It

250 years before women had won the right to vote! With a group of supporters, Elizabeth established a school for the children of the prisoners and brought about other humane changes to their conditions, such as women supervisors, proper prison clothing and the opportunity to learn reading and writing. There are many branches of the Elizabeth Fry Society active around the world today.

Rituals and Ceremonies

has put money into resources that leaders can use or individuals can download, and has posted stories of communities in Sierra Leone, the United States, England, and Germany, that are dealing with the problem of violence. Another program supported by the Council is the accompaniment program. The Council trains volunteers who go to violent places such as Israel and Palestine to witness the occupation there. It is similar to the Christian Peacemaker Teams, who go to war zones to "stand in the way" of violence.

Interpretations of Christianity have been responsible for crimes, such as the Spanish Inquisition, and also for good, such as helping to end slavery in the United States. Like most religions, Christianity has been a powerful force in the world.

Marriage

Marriage is seen as a sacred commitment between two loving people. Denominations vary in their marriage traditions. For example, some liberal churches encourage the couple to write their own vows; others do not. Some churches have a list of music that is considered acceptable; others are open to suggestions from the couple. Some churches will marry only a woman and man; others marry same-sex couples. Some will not marry people who have been divorced; for other churches, that is not a problem.

Rites of Passage

Baptism

Baptism comes from a Greek word meaning "to dip in water." Christians can be baptized by being sprinkled with water or dipped in a pool, lake or river. The ritual declares membership in the church and recalls how everyone is a child of God. For some Christians, baptism is a big celebration, with all the congregation (body of churchgoers) present, music, candles and lots of family members. Often the person wears special clothes for the occasion, usually white to symbolize purity. For other Christians, baptism is a quiet ceremony with few people present.

Most Christians are baptized as infants. In some denominations, young people are baptized when they are around 12 years old. There is no age limit. Jesus was baptized in the Jordan River by his cousin John when he was 30 years old. This marked the start of his ministry.

Confirmation

This ritual provides an opportunity for people to affirm their baptism and restate their desire to be a member of the Christian community. It can take place around puberty or any time later, but it always happens after a period of study and reflection. Confirmation is seen as a step towards maturity. Sometimes the person is anointed with holy oil, and often the religious leader and other members of the church will place their hands on the person and pray for them.

Young people wanting to be confirmed usually join a class to learn and to question what it means to grow in faith and be a mature Christian. These classes are also a time for people to get up-to-date information, compare ideas, talk about beliefs, life, death and discuss the place of Christianity in the world.

Golden Rule

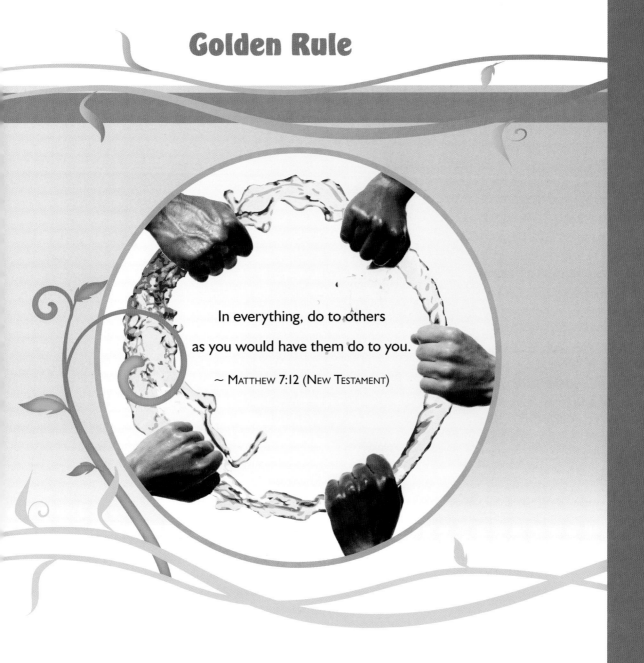

In everything, do to others
as you would have them do to you.

~ Matthew 7:12 (New Testament)

Chapter 7

Islam

Green Rule

Have you not considered how
Allah sets forth a parable of a
good word being like a good tree,
whose root is firm and whose
branches are in heaven?

~ Qur'an 14:24

Introducing: Farah Hattab

My name is Farah Hattab and I'm 17 years old. I'm in my first year of undergrad at the University of Calgary and hope to major in International Relations. Just like any other girl, I enjoy being with my friends. Whether it is sitting around together at home or going camping together, we can always find something to make us laugh. For the past three or four years, I have spent a lot of my free time volunteering in the Calgary Muslim community. Two years ago, a group of teenage girls and myself started an all-girls youth group, Young Muslimahs of Calgary. We meet weekly to discuss our day-to-day issues and how we can apply our own religion to help us find solutions to our concerns. Some of the things that we have done include:

- a number of summer camping trips all over Alberta;
- bake sales to raise money for our group;
- annual basketball tournaments;
- a bi-monthly bulletin at the Calgary Islamic Center, with articles written by members;
- mother and daughter events.

One of my new favourite hobbies that I started last year was snowboarding. I'm afraid of heights so it was a great accomplishment, and it now gives me something to look forward to for the cold winter.

Were you born in your religion or did you convert?

I am a born Muslim but wasn't a practising Muslim until the age of 15.

Briefly describe your home and family life.

I was born in Saudi Arabia, where I grew up for ten years, and then moved to Canada. However, my parents are originally from Palestine. I've never been there before but hope to visit it someday. I have two other sisters: Mayan, 19, and Yara, 12. We have been in Calgary now for almost nine years and it has truly become our home.

For you, what would make a great weekend?

Getting together with a bunch of friends for dinner at a restaurant (where we often make fools of ourselves) or at home and then watching movies or sharing stories.

What worries or concerns you about the world or your life these days?

My greatest concern today and tomorrow will be the way our religion, Islam, is being portrayed in the media. Since the attacks on September 11, 2001, our religion has been misrepresented and thousands of Muslims have been spiritually raped. One of the reasons I have been educating myself more about my religion is to spread the positive message about Islam so we can stop the hate in our societies. I do believe in the long run, this will just be a part of history, and we will no longer have to deal with it – just like women's rights or the African-American movement.

Where do you learn the stories and traditions in your religion?

I learn from family, friends and classes that I attend at the masjid (which is a place of worship). Also, at the U of C we have weekly classes that we attend, to listen to stories and speeches.

In what ways do you think your religion helps you live your life?

When something tries to ruin my day, like losing a wallet or not getting the grade on an exam, I think about the importance in our religion of patience and the rewards of heaven. We believe that everything is written by God, who wanted this to happen for me, and I need to accept it and take the lesson from it and move on with my life. For instance, I have lost my wallet several times, unfortunately, but I always say that maybe someone needed that money and my five or 20 dollars made them survive that day.

Have you ever been (or would you like to be) part of an interfaith event, worship or action?

Just this past week, I attended an interfaith event. Since it is the month of Ramadan, every year the Calgary Muslim community holds an event to bring people from all religions to come and break the fast with us. We had people from different parts of the world, such as Turkey and New Guinea, and other religions; the Catholic and Jewish communities in Calgary attended. It was a great experience, where you meet people from different beliefs and culture systems and exchange ideas and stories. I think we really get a positive atmosphere by the end of the night, where everyone gets a more positive picture about other countries and religions and helps to create peace within our city.

People have talked often about what divides people who practise different religions. What do you think could bring (or is bringing) religious people together?

I think, at the end of the day, we're all humans who want peace and security. That is our commonality in religions, so we can come together to share similar ideas and to accept differences because it is okay to be different. In the Qur'an, God says, "O mankind! We have created you from a male and female, and made you into nations and tribes, that you may know one another."

What is your wish for the youth of the world?

I think in most parts of the world, we are having a youth crisis. Unfortunately, a lot of teens are going down the path of drugs, alcohol, and unsafe sex. However, we still have a number of influential youth who will, God willing, help us change it for the coming generations. I hope, in the long run, more youth come together to speak of ways of making peace. I may sound unrealistic, but I think people at school have more respect for self-identity than in the past.

Do you have any advice for religious or other leaders in the world today?

I think we should go back to having a bit more religion in our governments because at least we will have something to refer to when it comes to social order.

What two or three things would you like people to know about your religion?

First, that we believe in only one all powerful and all knowing God, who is much greater than any human who has ever stepped foot on the universe. Second, I would like people to know that our Qur'an – a manual for humans that God and his messenger, the Prophet Muhammad, brought down for us – has never been changed, so it remains the same no matter how modernized or advanced our world becomes (no human will ever know more about the world than God). Most importantly, I would like people to know that our religion does not promote any kind of hate – in fact, one is not practising the right teachings of the Qur'an and the Prophet if they do.

Call to Kalma Prayer: Allahu Akbar

This is the Muslim call to prayer, which is sounded five times a day from mosques. Kalma means "prayer of faith," and Allahu Akbar means "God is the greatest."

God is the Greatest.

God is the Greatest.

God is the Greatest.

God is the Greatest.

I bear witness that there is no god but God.

I bear witness that there is no god but God.

I bear witness that Muhammad is
*   the messenger of God.*

I bear witness that Muhammad is
*   the messenger of God.*

Come to prayer.

Come to prayer.

Come to success.

Come to success.

God is the Greatest.

God is the Greatest.

There is no god but God.

A Story of Islam

A baby destined to change the world had a humble start in life in the city of Mecca. Before he was even born, around 570 CE, his father died. Soon after his birth, Amina, his poor mother, gave him into the care of a foster mother – a shepherd woman named Halima. At age three, Muhammad was reunited with his mother and his grandfather. His mother died when he was only six years old, and his grandfather passed away soon after, leaving him in the care of his uncle Abu

Thumbnail Sketch

Who is the founder?
Muhammad.

When did it start?
600 CE.

Are there any foundational sacred texts?
Qur'an (also spelled Koran); Hadith.

In what places do people worship? In mosques (also called masjids). Many people pray wherever they happen to be when the time for prayer comes.

Peace Be Upon Him

The name of the Prophet Muhammad is so highly regarded, that when Muslims say his name or write it, they usually add the blessing, "Peace be upon him." In writing, this is sometimes shortened to "pbuh." Some Muslims also add this blessing to other prophets, like Moses and Jesus.

Talib. Muhammad became a shepherd and later a trader. At age 25, he married his first wife. She was older than he by 15 years, but his beloved Khadija, a businesswoman, supported his work and his calling as long as she lived. While she lived, Muhammad did not marry other women.

Mecca at this time was a city of commerce where people from far and wide came to do business and exchange news. It was also a society where blood feuds could be carried on for generations, where violence was prevalent, where women were considered lesser beings, and where poverty claimed many lives. Mecca was also the site of the Kaabah, a shrine containing a sacred Black Stone. The Kaabah is believed to have been built by Ibrahim (also known as Abraham or Avraham) and his son Ishmael, and it was an ancient place of worship for Jews, Christians, and for people who worshipped idols and practised polytheism. The Kaabah was also a place

What are worship leaders called? Imams.

Where is the tradition practised? Mainly in Indonesia, the Middle East, Africa, Asia; most countries.

What are the main branches of the tradition? Sunni and Shi'ite.

Are there special holy days? The month of Ramadan, which is the ninth month in the lunar year, is considered holy because it is when the Qur'an was revealed to Muhammad. Ramadan is a time when Muslims focus on their faith. Eid ul-Fitr (the Festival of Fast-breaking) marks the end of the month. It is a celebration that includes gift-giving and feasting with family and friends. Other feasts include Eid ul-Adha (the Festival of Sacrifice) and Mawlid an-Nabi (Muhammad's birthday). The Muslim calendar is lunar.

The Five Pillars

The basic statements of faith for Muslims are contained in the Five Pillars.

1) **Shahada**: showing faith in one God; praying the *shahada* (which means "confession of faith") first thing in the morning and last thing at night.

2) **Salat**: observing prayer ritual five times each day: between first light and sunrise; just past mid-day; between mid-afternoon and sunset; between sunset and last daylight; and between darkness and dawn. Observing prayer in this way begins at around age ten.

of peace: at this site, enemies were required to lay down their weapons.

Muhammad often left his home to walk the hills and meditate. One day, he was sitting quietly in a cool cave. He was about 40 years old. Suddenly, he had a vision of the angel Gabriel (also called Jibril) who told him he'd been chosen to bring God's mes-sage to the people. "Recite!" the angel said.

Muhammad later told his family that the angel began to recite the Qur'an (meaning "word of God") to him. Muhammad memorized the words. He went home and taught the words to Khadija and their friends. Eventually, the words were written. For the rest of Muhammad's life, he received and transmitted these revelations. Most of the 114 chapters of the Qur'an include moral, social, and

Words to Know

Allah: "God" in Arabic.

Ayatullah: translates as "Sign of God"; a person who studies, teaches and gives guidance to the people.

Burqa or Chador: long coat and veil commonly worn outdoors by women in some Muslim societies.

Hadith: reports of Muhammad's life and teachings.

Halal: pure food; meat from animals killed in a respectful and humane manner. (It excludes shellfish and pork).

Hijab: a headscarf worn by some Muslim women.

Islam: translates as "submission to the will of God." It derives from the Arabic word for "peace," which is salaam.

Masjid: translates as "mosque"; a place of worship.

Muslim: a follower of Islam.

3) **Sawm:** abstaining from food, sex, smoking, or bodily pleasures during the daylight hours of the month of Ramadan.

4) **Zakat:** donating 2.5 % of personal savings to charity each year.

5) **Hajj:** making a pilgrimage to the holy city of Mecca (if physically able).

legal rules and directives. There are also proverbs, parables, and narratives, some of which are similar to those in the Bible and Torah.

The revelations changed everything. Muhammad had been given a heavy responsibility to challenge the society he lived in. The concept of only one God meant that polytheism and idol worship were wrong. The concept of one God for everyone meant that humans were really one family and that bloodlines and blood feuds were wrong too. The concept of one God loving men and women equally meant that viewing women as lesser beings could not be tolerated. And there was more to come.

Muhammad set out to teach this religion from a holistic perspective. He believed that political, economic, personal, legal, social, and spiritual values should be indivisible. He began a religion, and eventually an empire, that became bound up with conquest and expansion.

The religion was met with hostility by some and more than once Muham-

---

People of the Book: Muslims are the last of the three "People of the Book." Jews and Christians are the others who study scriptures that name Abraham as their father.

Polytheism: the worship of more than one god or goddess.

Sirah: the biography of Muhammad.

Sufi: a Muslim who seeks close, personal contact with Allah, usually described as a mystic. The most famous Sufi was the poet Rumi, who is very popular today and who has many works that have been translated into English.

Sunna: the "normative" way; words and deeds of the Prophet Muhammad.

Al Rashid: The First Mosque in North America

A teenaged bride from Lebanon didn't know what she was getting into when she married a trader bound for northern Canada in the 1930s. Temperatures that dipped well below zero, northern lights and neighbours who spoke English, Chipewyan, Yiddish and Cree were all new to her, as was the isolation from family. But Hilwe Hamdon met challenges with humour, faith and strength. She created a new family from her Canadian friends. Her home became a centre for people to gather, eat, and share stories and their faith. Hilwe's motto seemed to be "All are welcome."

Eventually, the Hamdon children needed higher education, and so the family moved south to Edmonton, the capital of Alberta, which was then a new province. With that accomplished, Hilwe next decided that there should be a mosque in Edmonton where people could pray, feast, marry, and hold funerals. Hilwe gathered the women and began the process. This was at a time when North America (and Europe) was in the midst of the terrible Great Depression. In western Canada, a

mad had to flee for his life. He left Mecca and established a safe community in Madina, which quickly attracted converts. Most of the people in the Arabian Peninsula converted to Islam before Muhammad's death in 632 CE. That same year, before his death, Muhammad returned with thousands of his followers to his birthplace, Mecca. He asked Muslims to continue making the pilgrimage each year – a practice that Muslims from all over the world continue to this day.

Within only 100 years after his death, Islam had spread all the way from Spain to India and had reached

into northern Africa. Because it spread so quickly and so far after Muhammad's death, the history of the growth of the religion is deep, wide, and sometimes confusing. It is filled with outbreaks of hostilities as the Muslim Empire grew. It is also filled with the great contributions to knowledge that affect life even today.

drought had caused farm lands to dry up and blow away; few people had jobs and there was little money anywhere. In spite of these conditions, the women approached the mayor of Edmonton and asked for land on which to build a mosque. The mayor said that if they could raise enough funds to build it, he'd get them land.

The women went door to door asking everyone for donations. Whether they were Jews, Muslims or Christians, shop owners and business people gave what they could. Slowly, the fund grew from a few dollars to $5,000 – just enough. The celebration to open Al Rashid on a cold December day in 1938 was in keeping with its multifaith beginning: among those present were Mayor John Fry of Edmonton, and Mayor I.F. Shaker of Hanna, Alberta, an Arab Christian. The mosque was the first built in North America.

For decades, Al Rashid was a gathering and worship place in the heart of the city, but in the early 1980s a larger mosque was built. One day, it was announced that the little mosque would be torn down to make way for a parking lot. It would have happened except that Hilwe Hamdon's grandchildren heard about it. Karen and Evelyn Hamdon gathered women, just as their grandmother and grand-aunt had done. With the sup-

port of the Canadian Council of Muslim Women, they went to city hall, wrote petitions and raised tens of thousands of dollars. Al Rashid was moved, restored and now stands among historic churches in Fort Edmonton Park. All are welcome.

Muslim scholars translated ancient Greek manuscripts and preserved and passed on these writings to European civilization. From the eighth to the 14th centuries, Muslim scholars laid the foundations for optical science, modern physics, chemistry, water-purification systems, and trigonometry. Unique architecture from that time is still greatly admired in places like India, Spain, and the Arab world. In medicine, the concepts of germs, cleanliness, and isolating infectious diseases were known, although these were unheard of in Europe at the time.

Eventually, the Muslim Empire was so vast that divisions appeared, for example between Arab Muslims and non-Arab Muslims, such as the Turks. At the same time, Europeans, mostly Christians, were divided amongst themselves too. In 1095, Pope Urban II made an effort to unite Christians in what is known as the Crusades.

Shari'ah Law

Shari'ah originally meant "a path to a virtuous life." Over many decades, its meaning has become layered by cultural interpretations and complex laws. Shari'ah laws affect family life, such as custody of children, divorce practices, dress codes, punishment for crimes such as theft or adultery, and the role and rights of women.

The laws were created as a code of living for Muslims, originally based on teachings from the Qur'an and the practices of the Prophet Muhammad. These laws are affected by the cultural practices and freedoms of the country in which they are applied. Shari'ah may be interpreted one way in Afghanistan and another way in the United States. For example, in some countries, the rights of women are protected in law and in custom; in other countries, women struggle for equality. This difference can affect how women are treated in a divorce or in their desire to get an education. In some

This was the time of knights rushing off to "save" Jerusalem from Islam. For about 300 years, periodic wars raged back and forth over the Holy Land.

In the 13th century, a new threat to the Muslim Empire appeared when the Tartars (Mongul tribes) attacked the Arabian Peninsula and eventually captured Baghdad, the Islamic capital. In a few years, though, many of them had settled and converted to Islam. Around this time, the Ottoman Empire was founded and within 100 years had taken control of vast areas of Asia and Europe. Between 1300 and World War I, this empire spread around the world, taking religion, culture, and systems of governance from Turkey to Portugal, Indonesia and beyond. Historically, Europe and the Ottoman Empire were suspicious of and sometimes hostile toward each other.

Today, Islam continues to grow. There is some resistance to this growth, but there are also welcoming signs of peace. One sign, for example, is the establishment of the Royal Institute for Interfaith Studies in Amman, Jordan. Another is the leadership of the Aga Khan and his foundation in the areas of health, education, civil society and the environment. The words spoken to a man in a cave near Mecca still echo down through the centuries and

countries, such as Iran, Shari'ah laws have become the laws of the land and are enforced by the courts.

Islam, like other religions, is affected by the customs of the country where it is practised. In Canada, for example, Shari'ah law is debated and discussed by people who relate it to the laws of the land and compare it to the rights and responsibilities of citizens protected by the Charter of Rights and Freedoms. The interpretation of Shari'ah laws is debated in many countries.

Rituals and Ceremonies

First and Last Words

The first words a baby hears are the call to prayer whispered by her or his father. The last words a person hears (if in the presence of other Muslims) are the call to prayer as a blessing into the next life.

Circumcision

It is customary, although not necessary, that males be circumcised (where the foreskin is cut from the penis) on the eighth day after birth. In some countries, particularly in Africa, some Muslims (also Christians) practise a controversial form of circumcision on young girls. This idea comes from culture rather than religion. It might be a ritual nick or it might take the form of debilitating genital mutilation, where the entire clitoris is cut away. Female genital mutilation is outlawed in most of the world.

Jihad

Jihad means "striving in the cause of God" or "holy struggle." One interpretation of this word is internal struggle, like when we are fighting temptation. Another jihad is external, such as in the defense of Islam against an aggressor. If conflict is involved, the rule is that the jihad must be defensive, not offensive.

The media in the West has often misunderstood its meaning; jihad is not about converting people through violence. Muhammad said, "The most excellent jihad is when one speaks a true word in the presence of a tyrannical ruler."

Rites of Passage

Fourth-year Celebration

A celebration takes place when a child first reads from the Qur'an, which usually happens at about the age of four.

There are no special rites of passage or coming-of-age ceremonies for Muslim youth.

☀ Golden Rule

Not one of you truly believes
until you wish for others what
you wish for yourself
~ HADITH

Chapter 8

Sikhism

Green Rule

Air is the Guru, Water is the Father
and Earth is the Great Mother of All.

~ Siri Guru Granth Sahib

Introducing: Arvind Singh Bhatia

My name is Arvind Singh Bhatia. I am 17 years old and am currently in grade 12 at Lester B. Pearson High School. My hobbies are playing and watching sports (hockey, soccer, basketball, etc.). I enjoy spending time with my family and friends. I also enjoy dancing (bhangra — a cultural dance established many years ago in Punjab).

Were you born into your religion or did you convert?

I was very fortunate to be born into Sikhism. It is something I am very proud of and have a lot of interest in.

Briefly describe your home and family.

I was born in Calgary, Alberta. I have lived in Calgary my whole life and really enjoy it in this wonderful and booming city. I have eight members in my family: parents, grandparents, two brothers and one sister (and myself).

What worries or concerns you about the world or your life these days?

The thing I am greatly concerned with nowadays is the growing racism and violence. I believe racism should be completely removed from this world. We all need to live in a society full of love and peace. I am also very concerned about the growing violence in schools, especially after what happened in [a recent college shooting in] Montreal and the many other cases after that, which have taken place in the United States. Before schools used to be a safe place where parents could send their children and not worry about their safety, but nowadays schools have become even more dangerous. Something needs to be done to put a stop to this before it gets out of hand and innocent students and teachers are targeted.

Where do you learn the stories and traditions in your religion?

I started attending Khalsa School when I was five years old. Khalsa School is held every Saturday from 2 p.m. to 5 p.m. During this time, we learned Kirtan (the performing of Sikh hymns) using the vaja (harmonium) and tabla (East Indian percussion instrument). We were also taught the recitation of Gurbani [sacred scripture]; reading, writing and speaking the Punjabi language; and Sikh history. During Sikh history class, we were taught the teachings of our gurus.

In what ways do you think your religion helps you live your life?

I think my religion plays a major role in helping me live my life. I am a strict vegetarian, meaning I do not eat meat or eggs. I think this is probably something I always get asked by others; they ask me how I can live without meat. My answer is, "Simple, I have never tried meat before so therefore I do not know what it tastes like." One of the most important things to me is my identity. Since I keep my hair, I have always stood out in a crowd of people. I feel that this is what separates a Sikh from any other person, making Sikhs around the world very unique. Many people have asked me, what is that on your head? and why do you wear it? Instead of getting mad and saying, what is it to you? I explain to them that my religion requires me to keep my hair. We keep our hair, knowing it is a gift from God.

Are there ways that your religion is a problem for you?

So far, I have not had any problem with my religion. Instead there is something new I learn about it every day, which inspires me to keep learning more. The true meaning of Sikh is "a person who learns."

People have talked often about what divides people who practise different religions. What do you think could bring (or is bringing) religious people together?

Personally, I believe the new generation is very open-minded. They don't have the same problems with people of different religions as much as older people do. Living in Canada, I do not find this as big of a problem as compared to other countries. I think the fact that Canada is so multicultural helps people understand others from different religions and backgrounds. A solution to this problem would be an urge to spread the message of peace and unity among everyone, so we can all live in a peaceful society.

What is your wish for the youth of the world?

I wish for the youth of today to work together to build a better and safer society. I feel nowadays people, teenagers in particular, are highly influenced by their peers and the world around them. Drugs and alcohol are a growing problem, from which no one benefits. We need to work together and be responsible role models for the new generations to come.

Do you have any advice for religious or other leaders in the world today?

The only advice I think I can give would be to follow your religion the best you can.

What two or three things would you like people to know about your religion?

The most important thing about Sikhism, according to me, would be the three golden rules recited by our first guru, Nanak Dev Ji. Wherever Guru Nanak Dev Ji went, he told people these three golden rules so that they could follow a path of honesty and hard work:

1) Nap Japana — Recite God's name (remember God at all times).
2) Kirat Karni — Live an honest living (do not cheat others).
3) Vand Kay Chacna — Share with others (do not be selfish).

Sikhism is based on equality. There is no such thing as status, colour, or race. Everyone is considered equal, no matter what religion they are.

Anand Sahib (Prayer)

This prayer, written by the third guru, Amar Das, is said at the end of the service in the gurdwara.

Listen to my joy, my fortunate friends. All my desires have been fulfilled. I have reached God, the supreme spirit, and all my sorrows have vanished. Sorrow, affliction and suffering have been relieved through hearing the true word. Saints and holy people are glad on hearing it from the perfect Guru. Pure are the hearers; stainless the speakers. The true Guru will fill their hearts. Nanak says, heavenly trumpets sound for those who bow at the Guru's feet.

~ Siri Guru Granth Sahib 40

A Story of Sikhism

Five hundred years ago, a village couple welcomed their baby boy into the world. It was a full-moon night in mid-April 1469 in Talwindi, northern India. The couple named the boy Nanak.

Stories about Nanak tell us that he was a thoughtful child who was curious about spiritual matters from an early age. His Hindu family taught him the ways of their tradition, and he also watched the religious practices of

Thumbnail Sketch

Who is the founder? Guru Nanak.

When did it start? 1500 CE.

Are there any foundational sacred texts? Siri Guru Granth Sahib, Dasam Granth and Janam Sakhis.

In what places do people worship? At home in front of a copy of the Siri Guru Granth Sahib and in the gurdwara or temple. Gurdwaras are open at all times and to all people.

What are worship leaders are called? Granthi.

The Five Ks (The Five Articles of Faith)

The Five Ks help Sikhs to identify themselves and to remember what it is to live as a Sikh.

1) One should not cut his or her *kes* (or "hair," which can also include beards. Men and some women wear their hair in a top knot and wrap a turban around it.)

2) One should carry a *kangha* (or "comb").

3) One should carry a *kirpan* (or "short sword").

4) One should wear special *kacch* (or "underwear").

5) One should wear a *kara* (or "steel bracelet").

his Muslim neighbours. He wondered about the differences and similarities of the two ways of life and how each tradition helped people in their daily lives. A story about eight-year-old Nanak tells how his dad gave him money to run an errand for him. Along the way, Nanak saw some *sadhu*, Hindu holy people. Nanak used his father's money to buy food to give them. When he was a teenager, Nanak received enough money from his father to start a business, but again he spent all he had to buy food for holy men. "They were men of God," he told his father, "and they were in need."

Eventually, Nanak went to work in a business owned by Muslims and there learned not only about the business but much about Islam as well. At age 19, he married Sulakhni, a Hindu woman of his (business) caste, and together they had two sons. But Nanak's curiosity and deep thinking about spiritual mat-

Where is the tradition practised? Mainly in India, North America and Britain; worldwide.

What are the main branches of the tradition? Indian Sikhs (who mostly use the Punjabi language) and American Sikhs (who use English and some Punjabi and who refer to themselves as "3HO" – Healthy, Happy, Holy Organization).

Are there special holy days? Divali, in November or early December, is the festival of lights, when Sikhs tell the story of when the sixth guru was released from prison and people in the city of Amritsar lit lamps to welcome him home. The Baisakhi festival marks the anniversary of the founding of the Khalsa. Gurpurb is a festival in honour of a guru. The gurpurb for Guru Nanak, in November, has processions, singing and food sharing. The tenth guru, Gobind Singh, is celebrated in December with sports and games. The martyrdoms of the fifth and ninth gurus are remembered in summer with gurpurbs that include storytelling, processions and worship. Communities make their own decisions about the exact date on which to hold festivals. Sikhs follow a lunar calendar.

Sikh Code of Conduct

- Abstain from using tobacco or other intoxicants.
- Never cut the hair on any part of the body.
- Do not eat meat.
- Refrain from any sexual contact outside of marriage.
- Wear the Five Ks.

ters consumed him. One day, when he was in his 30s, he went to the river to bathe as he did every morning. There he had vision that changed his life.

In the vision, God gave Nanak responsibility for teaching people about the divine path that would lead them to God. For three days, Nanak did not appear at home, and when he finally did, it was to make a pronouncement and to say goodbye. What he said puzzled everyone around him – "There is neither Hindu nor Muslim." What he meant was that to God, everyone is the same. And so he became Guru Nanak, a teacher. He spent the next 20 years travelling throughout India, as well as Saudi Arabia, Iraq, Iran, Afghanistan, Pakistan, Tibet, and the island of Sri Lanka.

Guru Nanak drew from some of the ideas in Islam (such as the belief that there is only one God) and Hinduism (such as the beliefs about karma and reincarnation), but he had new and creative ideas about spirituality and how to live in the world in a good way. He disagreed strongly with the caste system and preached that it

Words to Know

Dasam Granth: book of the tenth guru, which contains mythology and poetry important to Guru Gobind Singh.

Guru: a servant of God who, through his or her teachings, leads people to God.

Janam Sakhis: contains stories about Guru Nanak's life.

Karma: the law of cause and effect; the belief that people are responsible for their own destiny.

Khalsa: the community of the pure; the brother and sisterhood of "soldier-saints." The Khalsa was begun by the tenth guru, Gobind Singh.

Langar: a free meal given to everyone after the worship service in the gurdwara.

The Golden Temple

The Golden Temple is the most well-known gurdwara in the world. It is located in Amritsar (in the Punjab), India. Built in the middle of a sacred lake, the temple has four separate entrances. They symbolize that all four castes are welcome in this house of God.

should be abolished. He believed that women were equal with men. He used his poetic talents to write great hymns and poems expressing his deep belief in one God. He believed that all human beings could have direct access to God and that everyone is equal before God.

These are spiritual ideas that, when put into action, can be liberating for some and threatening for others. For example, if the caste system were abolished and the "untouchables" (people from the lowest caste) gained freedom to be educated, who would do the dirty labour that kept society going? If women were free to lead worship and interpret the scriptures, what might happen to the power of men? At the time (in some places, this practice still exists), it was tradition that when a man died, the widow would commit *sati*, throwing herself on the funeral pyre (the burning pile on which the corpse was burned). Nanak forbade this practice and encouraged widows to remarry. Another practice at the time was to allow girl babies to die in infancy if the couple had wanted a boy. Nanak forbade this practice too, and, in fact, forbade Sikhs to even associate with anyone who killed a baby.

Manji: the stool on which the Siri Guru Granth Sahib (holy book) is placed in the gurdwara

Mool Mantar: means "basic teaching" and refers to what Sikhs teach about God.

Ragi: Sikh musician.

Rebirth: the idea that the soul does not die with the body but is born again and again; reincarnation.

Sewa: service to others; preparing and serving the langar is part of this service.

Sikh: (pronounced seek) learner, disciple or follower.

Siri Guru Granth Sahib: the holy book containing Guru Nanak's hymns and theology, writings and songs of other gurus, as well as prayers and writings of Hindu and Muslim holy men.

How the Khalsa began

In the days of the tenth guru, Gobind Singh, there was great suffering of the people who tried to follow the Sikh way of life. This was a new religion in India and it was met by some with suspicion and by others with violence. After the martyrdom and fighting in the late 1600s, Gobind Singh believed that Sikhs needed to do something more to protect themselves. He called together Sikh warriors. He told them that he believed that God had asked for the faithful to completely surrender themselves to defend their faith. He asked "Are there five among you who are willing to die for the Sikh cause?" No one spoke for a long time and the guru waited with patience. Finally, one person stepped forward. The guru led him into his tent; the crowd heard a thud and saw the guru come out of the tent. There was blood on his sword.

Again he asked, "Who among you is willing to die for the Sikh cause?" After a long silence, another man stepped

In his early 50s, Guru Nanak stopped travelling and settled in Kartarpur, northern India. People flocked to listen and learn. Some even moved there. These were the first Sikhs. An important part of Guru Nanak's belief and practice was to feed all who were hungry. It was in Kartarpur where the practice of the langar began, where people of any caste could eat together. Before he died in 1539, the guru named his successor to carry on the teachings. This began the line of nine more gurus.

Each of the nine gurus who followed continued the teachings started by Guru Nanak and each brought something new to the religion. The following list highlights the contributions of each guru.

1539–1552

Guru Angad focused on language, literacy for young and old, and the building of gurdwaras.

1552–1574

Guru Amar Das emphasized the importance of women preachers.

1574–1581

Guru Ram Das was a builder and the poet who wrote the hymns that are sung at Sikh weddings.

1581–1606

Guru Arjan built the Golden Temple. Following the suspicion and struggle brought about by

forward and was led into the tent. Again, and twice more, a volunteer followed the guru; the crowd heard a thud and saw fresh blood on the sword in the guru's hand. After the fifth volunteer followed the guru into the tent, the guru did not come out alone. All five of the men stood before the crowd, unharmed, dressed in beautiful yellow clothes and holding a special sword.

These five men were the first initiates into the first Khalsa, the brotherhood of soldier-saints.

the introduction of his new ideas, Guru Arjan was arrested and put to death in 1606.

1606–1644

Guru Har Gobind, the son of Guru Arjan, believed that Sikhs needed to be able to defend themselves and began training Sikhs as soldiers.

1644–1661

Guru Har Rai, the grandson of Guru Har Gobind (all four of Har Gobind's sons were dead), tried to make peace between Muslims and Sikhs, but the fighting continued.

1661–1664

Guru Har Krishan, the son of Guru Har Rai, became Guru at only five years of age. He lived during an epidemic of smallpox, although he cured many people through prayer and blessing, he himself died of smallpox at age eight.

1664–1675

Guru Tegh Bahadur gave his life defending the right of Hindus and Sikhs to worship freely. He was arrested and given the option of giving up his religion, but he refused. He was beheaded.

1675–1708

Guru Gobind Singh was only a child when he was named guru, but he grew up to become the most influential leader after Guru Nanak. He instituted the Five K's and the Khalsa. (See sidebars on each of these topics in this chapter.) Before he died in 1708, he said that in the future, the scriptures and the community would serve as guru, and so he was the last of ten gurus to shape the religion.

The Khalsa

This passage comes from a Sikh code of conduct.

He or she is of the Khalsa, who is absorbed in God's name.

He or she is of the Khalsa, who is devoted to the Guru.

He or she is of the Khalsa, who speaks evil of no one.

He or she is of the Khalsa, who conquers evil passions.

He or she is of the Khalsa, who stands by the oppressed.

After 200 years of guru leadership, things changed again for Sikhs. Persecution increased and gurdwaras were either closed or cared for by Hindus. But in 1849, Sikhs enjoyed more religious freedom after the British took control of the Punjab. One hundred years later, Gandhi led the Indian people to freedom from the British. One result of this was that Pakistan, a country for Muslims, was created. The border between Pakistan and India cut through the middle of the Punjab – right through the area where most Sikhs lived. They rioted when they were forced to leave Pakistan so that it could be a Muslim country. The result was that thousands of people died. Many Sikhs dreamed of having their own country. (To this day, unrest still exists in this part of the world.)

About this time, many Sikhs began moving to Europe and Britain. In the 1960s, the British Sikh Missionary Society was formed for the purpose of teaching others about the religion.

The foundations of cooperation and interfaith dialogue, laid down by Guru Nanak in the very beginning, have helped Sikhs take leadership in organizations devoted to bringing religions together. Sikh scriptures contain the holy writings of Sikhs as well as of Muslims and Hindus. Guru Nanak taught that God dwells within us "like the image in a mirror." Many Sikhs in North America have moved easily into the work of interfaith communities, helping to heal people and the planet.

He or she is of the Khalsa, who does not covet another's wife, husband or wealth.

He or she is of the Khalsa, who rides a fiery steed.

He or she is of the Khalsa, who fights in the vanguard.

He or she is of the Khalsa, who is as hard as steel.

He or she is of the Khalsa, who dies for his or her faith.

~ Sikh Rahit Nama

Rituals and Ceremonies

Birth Ritual

Soon after a baby is born, he or she will hear the Mool Mantar, the first words from the Siri Guru Granth Sahib. Relatives and friends visit and bring gifts for the baby. The parents offer their guests sweets or small presents to show their happiness.

Naming Ceremony

When a baby is a few weeks old, the parents take him or her to the gurdwara for the naming ceremony. The final prayer of the regular service includes prayers for the baby and family, and thanksgiving for the birth. The parents lay the child in front of the Siri Guru Granth Sahib, and the granthi opens the book and chooses a verse at random to read for the baby. The first letter of the verse's first word will become the first letter of the child's name. Sometimes it is the responsibility of the grandparents to name the child.

Special hymns are sung for the baby, including the words, "May God the Guru be kind to you. May you love the company of God's people. May God robe you with honour and may your food be the singing of God's praises."

Boy babies may also receive the last name Singh which means "lion," and girl babies may receive the last name Kaur which means "princess" or "lioness." This tradition began with the tenth guru, Gobind Singh, who wanted Sikhs to stop using their other last names because, in India, last names indicate caste and Sikhs do not believe in the caste system.

The granthi may also perform the special ceremony during which the baby and mother drink amrit ("nectar" or, alternatively, sugar water) and the granthi prays for the child. Sometimes the baby receives his or her first kara, the steel bracelet that is one of the Five Ks.

Rites of Passage

Preparing for Marriage

Traditionally, marriages were arranged by the families of young people, but today there have been some changes. The families are usually still involved, but the young people often have a say in the choice of their husband or wife, and they will have dated at least a few times. It is important that the families know one another. The marriage will not take place unless both bride and groom agree to it.

The First Turban

When a boy is small, he may wear a simple cloth head covering called a *patka*. When he is around 12 years old, the family will ask the *granthi* ("guru" or worship leader) to tie the first turban on his head at a special honour ceremony. *Ardas* (or "prayers") are chanted for the boy in the presence of the Siri Guru Granth Sahib.

Amrit Ceremony

When a Sikh is old enough to understand what it means to join the Khalsa (pledge to follow the Sikh code of conduct), the Amrit Ceremony is held. Both men and women may join.

Golden Rule

No one is my enemy, none is
a stranger, and everyone is my
friend.

– Siri Guru Granth Sahib 1299

Chapter 9

Bahá'i Faith

Green Rule

Know thou that every created thing is
a sign of the revelation of God.

~ GLEANINGS FROM THE WRITINGS

OF BAHÁ'U'LLÁH 177

Introducing: Maren Stachnik

My name is Maren Stachnik. I am 16 years old and in the 11th grade. I was born and raised in Calgary, Alberta. Music is a big part of my life. I am currently taking grade nine piano and have been playing for about ten years. I also enjoy singing. I used to play the flute and the cello, but piano and voice are the only things I've had the time to continue with. I was also very active in musical theatre. I belonged to the Alberta Bahá'í Youth Theatre Company and also participated in musicals at my school. A few of my interests include cooking, travelling, the outdoors and sports. I love to cook and have been watching cooking shows since I was a little kid. One of my greatest passions and interests is travelling. I love to learn about different cultures and experience different music, food and celebrations in different countries. So far, I have been to the United States, Mexico, France, Italy, Germany and Israel. I am also hoping to attend university in Australia. I also enjoy listening to all types of music. I like popular music, country, R & B, hip hop, techno and house music, jazz, reggae, Latin and African music. I really like to play sports, but I don't play for any organized teams. I like to stay active. And I love to learn and try new things.

Were you born into your religion or did you convert?

I was born into my religion.

Briefly describe your home and family.

I am from a family of five. I have two older siblings: a sister who is 22 and a brother who is 19. Neither of them lives at home anymore. My sister is going to university in Edmonton and my brother lives in his own apartment. He is working to save money to become a paramedic. I also have two dogs. I live in Calgary, in an average neighbourhood, in a pretty average house. My dad works as a financial analyst for a big oil company, and my mom is a social worker.

For you, what would make a great weekend?

A great weekend would have a balance of both nice and relaxing activities but also fun ones. I like to be able to do something with my friends but also have time to relax at home. I enjoy going out with my friends from school, but often there is drinking involved. I don't like to be around that so I also enjoy going out with the kids that I know from my own religion. Then I don't have pressures to worry about drinking and so on.

Would you like to mention what worries or concerns you have about the world or your life these days?

I think society in general has got me pretty worried. It's funny to think that kids these days complain about not having a new iPod while the kids in Africa don't even have water to drink. Society in North America is definitely going downhill. The materialism that we see every day is getting out of control. Most of society is based on getting materialistic things like money, clothes, cars, looks and entertainment. How is it that actors and actresses get paid more than teachers who educate our children? You can't turn on the television without getting advertisement after advertisement on how you're not perfect unless you have a particular product. Teenagers these days are pegged with stereotypes about not having any morals, only wanting to party, have sex, drink, smoke or do drugs. But with all of these huge corporations and companies trying to target youth's insecurities and vulnerabilities to sell them useless products and standards, just to make money, I don't think that they are the only ones without morals.

Where do you learn the stories and traditions in your religion?

I mostly just grew up with them. I learned them when I was little at children's education classes or when my mom and dad told them to me. Sometimes we talked about them at suppertime or just when we were sitting and talking.

In what ways do you think your religion helps you live your life?

When I tell people I don't drink or do drugs or that I will try to remain chaste, a lot of them think that I am too sheltered and naive. But I think the guidelines I get from my religion protect me from a very difficult, scary lifestyle. My religion shapes the way I live my life and what I choose to do. It teaches me what really matters in life. Over and above all the materialistic things is the importance of trying to live a better life, be a better person and help other people.

Are there ways that your religion is a problem for you?

The way religion is portrayed now is very negative. It's not "cool" to be spiritual or be religious. I find that I keep a certain wall up because I'm afraid if people knew that I was spiritual or that I believe in God that they wouldn't accept me. I think that the fact that the media barely portrays religion at all assists with this unawareness of God and religion in society. But when it does portray it, it's normally extreme and out of context. This definitely causes the "uncool" stereotype. So it isn't my religion that is a problem for me but people's perception of who I am if I admit to being as religious as I am.

Does your religion have anything special to say to teens or children?

The Bahá'í faith holds youth and children in a very high regard. They believe that youth have huge difficulties facing them, but they will rise to shape the future and the world to what it could be. Actually, the faith believes that it is the youth who will change the world and not adults.

I do belong to a youth group. Only I wouldn't call it a youth group, I would instead call it a group of youth. We get together, have fun, pray and learn the [sacred] Writings. We share the same goals, and I get a lot of support from the youth and really great friendships. Right now we are working on a project to bring moral teachings to a group of junior youth in a low-income area of the city. We all work really hard and cooperatively. I think the experience has been almost life-changing for me. I guess it taught me that I really can make a difference.

Have you ever been (or would you like to be) part of an interfaith event, worship or action?

I don't think I have ever been part of one but I guess it would be a nice experience.

People have talked often about what divides people who practice different religions. What do you think could bring (or is bringing) religious people together?

I think it is religious differences that divide people, and I think in time that that division will end. I think more universal religious awareness would be a good idea. People don't know about other religions, so they don't know how similar they are to their own. I think all religions talk about being a better person and helping other people. It would be good to perhaps celebrate more religious holidays. For instance, instead of just having Christmas and Easter off, we could have other sacred holidays of different religions recognized, such as Hanukkah or Ramadan. It's a small thing, but it could create more religious awareness.

What is your wish for the youth of the world?

I wish that the youth of the world don't give into the pre-set standards of society and try to rise above the negative stereotypes of youth and dare to be different.

Do you have any advice for religious or other leaders in the world today?

I find, for me personally, that to lead by example is better than trying to tell people there is a better way to live. All leaders in the world will become leaders if they are positive examples for everyone.

What two or three things would you like people to know about your religion?

I would like them to know that it has answers for today's questions about whether we should do things or not, for example drinking. I would like them to know that the laws I follow are important and make sense. They provide me with a freedom from a scary lifestyle and other problems. I would also like them to know that it isn't weird even though it sounds unfamiliar.

A Prayer

I bear witness, O my God, that Thou hast created me to know Thee and to worship Thee. I testify at this moment, to my powerlessness and to Thy might, to my poverty and to Thy wealth. There is none other God but Thee, the Help in Peril, the Self-Subsisting.

~ Daily obligatory prayer from Prayers and Meditations by Bahá'u'lláh

A Story of Bahá'í

In the 1840s, when the earliest postage stamp was used and the first telegraph made instant electronic communication possible, there lived a 25-year-old man in Persia who believed that God called him to communicate a message of great importance. Siyyid 'Ali Muhammad Shirazi was a Muslim who knew that it would be risky to speak out. The society he lived in was strictly controlled; he knew that political and religious leaders might see his words as a challenge to their authority and way of life. He believed that God wanted all religions to unite and wrote about this in a book he

Thumbnail Sketch

Who are the founders?
The Báb and Bahá'u'lláh.

When did it start?
1844 CE.

Where did it start? Persia (now called Iran).

Are there any foundational sacred texts? The Most Holy Book, the Book of Certitude, the Seven Valleys and the Hidden Words.

In what places do people worship? In homes and community centres; also in seven temples worldwide.

Bahá'í Teaching on Animals

Train your children from their earliest days to be infinitely tender and loving to animals.

If an animal be sick, let the children try to heal it; if it be hungry, let them feed it;

if thirsty, let them quench its thirst; if weary, let them see that it rests.

~ Joel Beversluis, ed. *Sourcebook of the World's Religions: An Interfaith Guide to Religion and Spirituality* (Novato, CA: New World Library, 2000).

called *The Bayan*. He believed that God was sending someone to open the way for a new religion and that the human family would live in peace if they listened to this person. Siyyid 'Ali Muhammad knew the stories of others who had gone against the status quo – people like Abraham, Buddha, Jesus, Krishna and Muhammad. He also knew how their messages were received by their societies: some welcomed them; many didn't want to be challenged; some viewed them as heretics.

But this merchant believed that he had a holy mission to announce the arrival of the one who would fulfill the prophetic expectations of all the great religions. Because he believed that his mission was to "open the gate" for this promised one, Siyyid 'Ali Muhammad became known as the Báb. One by one, 17 men and one woman came to recognize the Báb and believe his message. Together with the Báb, this group became known as the Letters of the Living. As other people converted and the movement grew, so did the danger. These Bábis even claimed that the one who was coming would be the new prophet of God. But the prevailing Muslim belief was that Muhammad was the last prophet. The Bábis,

What are worship leaders called? There is no priesthood. Any member of the community can lead worship.

Where is the Faith practised? Iran, India, Europe, Africa and around the world.

Are there special holy days? Ayyám-Ha is the preparation for the Feast of Ridván, which commemorates Bahá'u'lláh's announcement that he was a prophet. These days are set aside for

special acts of charity, gift-giving, and preparing for the Bahá'í Fast. (See "The Bahá'í Fast" in this chapter.) They occur from late February to early March. The Declaration of the Báb

commemorates the day when the Báb announced that a great messenger of God would soon arrive to usher in an era of world peace. It takes place on May 23. Naw Ruz is the Bahá'í New Year, on

March 21 – the spring equinox. This is also the day when the Bahá'í calendar begins.

The Bahá'í Fast

Bahá'ís do not eat or drink anything from sunrise to sunset for 19 consecutive days from March 2 to March 20 each year. Known simply as "the Fast," this time for renewal comes before the Bahá'í New Year and provides an opportu-

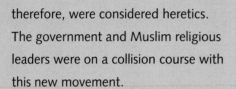

therefore, were considered heretics. The government and Muslim religious leaders were on a collision course with this new movement.

Arrests, persecution, and torture of these believers began. Six years after the Báb first spoke out, he was arrested, tortured, and killed by a firing squad. He was 31 years old. One story about that day is that when the soldiers arrived to take him to the place of execution, he told them he was still giving instructions to one of his followers. They took him anyway. When he was shot by the firing squad, he disappeared from sight. The soldiers found him back in his prison cell still talking with his follower. When he saw them return, he said, "I am ready now." And so, he was taken a second time to die.

Violence increased following the martyrdom of the Báb and an attempted assassination on the Shah, the leader of Persia. In the course of two years, 20,000 people died in the violence. Many were tortured and imprisoned, among them someone called Mirza Husayn-'Ali-i-Nuri.

Mirza Husayn-'Ali was 28 years old. His father was a nobleman in the Shah's court in Tehran, the capital of Persia. Theirs was a wealthy Muslim family, and Mirza Husayn-'Ali was expected to take advantage of the opportunities open to him and become part of the Shah's world. But from his youth, he seemed to have other things on his mind. He was known for his intelligence, generosity, and kindness. He took his Muslim religion seriously and

Words to Know

Allah'u'Abha: a phrase that translates as, "God is most glorious!" This is a common greeting used by Bahá'í s.

The Báb: one of the founders of the Bahá'í Faith whose name translates as "the Gateway to God."

Bábis: people who followed the Báb.

Bahá'í: (pronounced ba-HI) comes from an Arabic word meaning "glory" or "splendour."

Bahá'u'lláh: (pronounced ba-HOW-la) one of the founders of the Bahá'í faith whose name translates as "Glory to God."

nity to think about personal spiritual progress toward harmony, peace, and justice. It's a time to detach and not worry about the material world, and to think about the poor and hungry in the world. Believers get up before dawn to pray and have breakfast. Nursing or pregnant mothers, the ill, the very young or very old are not required to take part in the fast.

asked questions of his tutors. What was God like? Why was there such poverty? Why were men and women treated differently?

In 1835, when he was 18 years old, Mirza Husayn-'Ali married Asiyih Navvab. The couple became known as "the Father of the Poor" and "the Mother of Consolation" for their generosity and compassion to the poor. Asiyih became the mother of seven children, three of whom lived to be adults. Their first child, 'Abdu'l-Baha (whose name means "servant of God"), was born in 1844, the same year that the Báb made his prophetic declaration. As was the custom, Mirza Husayn-'Ali married again, this time to Fatimih Mahdi-i-Ulya in 1849 in Tehran. They eventually had six children of whom four survived.

When Mirza Husayn-'Ali heard the Báb's ideas about unity among the religions, they made sense to him. He committed himself to the Báb, and the Báb gave him the title Bahá'u'lláh. But he didn't assume this title right away. After the execution of the Báb in 1850 and the subsequent horrors of the assassination attempt and riots, Mirza Husayn-'Ali was imprisoned and tortured in a notorious underground prison. It was in this dark and terrible prison that he had a profound spiritual experience in which he said he was visited by a maiden of God. She told him that his life's mission was to spread the vision of a new-world order and to lead the world toward peace. He believed that he was the prophet foretold in the scriptures of Zoroastrians, Jews,

The Bayan: This book, written by the Báb, promotes a worldwide law that would replace and fulfill the laws and codes set out by previous religious leaders like Moses, Buddha, Jesus, and Muhammad. It also predicts that a great prophet would come to establish this law.

Bahá'í Morals

To uphold a high moral standard, Bahá'u'lláh stressed
- honesty
- trustworthiness
- chastity outside marriage
- service to others
- purity of motive
- generosity
- deeds over words
- unity
- work as a form of worship

Bahá'ís follow the moral code of the Ten Commandments. In addition, Bahá'u'lláh stressed avoiding
- killing
- stealing
- lying
- adultery and promiscuity
- gambling
- alcoholic drinks
- drug abuse
- gossip and backbiting

~ *The Bahá'ís: A Profile of the Bahá'í Faith and Its World-wide Community.* NewYork: Office of Public Information of the Baha'i International Community, 1994, 32.

Christians and Muslims, and that all religions were one under God. After four months in prison, he was sent into exile along with his family and followers to the city of Baghdad in Iraq. (Baghdad was then part of the Ottoman Empire.) He never returned home again.

In Baghdad, Mirza Husayn-'Ali wrote the first of several books: the *Seven Valleys*, the *Four Valleys*, *Hidden Words*, and the *Book of Certitude*. It was during this time that he confessed to his followers and eldest son that he was the one to whom the Báb had referred as prophet. He was the one sent by God to bring together the world religions and to establish a new-world order of peace and justice, but he was not ready to proclaim this to the public. His work in Baghdad consisted of building the community, writing, and teaching. Here, he married a third wife, Gawhar Khanum, who bore him a daughter.

But after ten years, his influence grew too strong. The religious leaders

Principles Emphasized by Bahá'u'lláh

- The oneness of humanity
- The equality of women and men
- The elimination of prejudice
- The elimination of extremes of wealth and poverty
- The independent investigation of truth
- Universal education
- Religious tolerance
- The harmony of science and religion
- A world commonwealth of nations
- A universal second language

of Baghdad told him to leave. Exiled again, this time to Constantinople (now Istanbul, Turkey), he prepared for the journey. Just outside Baghdad, Mirza Husayn-'Ali and his followers stayed in the Garden of Ridván for 12 days. It was in this place that he assumed the title given to him by the Báb. He became Bahá'u'lláh.

After a short stay in Constantinople, Bahá'u'lláh was sent to Adrianople (now Edirne, Turkey), where he continued teaching. It was from here that he began writing to queens, kings, presidents, emperors, and prime ministers urging them to lead their people into a world order of peace. The letters proclaimed the coming unification of humanity and the emergence of a world civilization. From here Bahá'u'lláh, his family, and followers were exiled again, sailing the Mediterranean to Alexandria, Egypt, and then finally to the city of Acre, Israel, in 1868. In prison there, he wrote the central book for the Bahá'í laws and his main literary work,

the *Most Holy Book*. He lived in and around Acre under house arrest or in prison until his death in 1892 at age 74.

After his passing, 'Abdu'l-Baha, Bahá'u'lláh's first son and confidant, became leader of the movement and the interpreter of his father's writings. Finally free of a life of imprisonment, he began a series of international speaking tours and travelled to France, Britain, Germany, Hungary, and North America by 1912. He settled in Haifa, Israel, and wrote his major book *Tablets of the Divine Plan,* which is about spreading the faith worldwide. His eldest grandson, Shoghi Effendi, became the next leader of the community and devoted his life to expanding the faith. He translated the scriptures into English and, under his leadership, the Bahá'ís established a presence at the United Nations in New York City.

Shoghi Effendi continued to promote the ideals of the faith, teaching that all religions should be embraced equally because they all come from the

Bahá'í Houses of Worship

Unlike most religions, Bahá'ís do not build many houses of worship. There are seven such temples in the world: in India, the US, Panama, Australia, Uganda, Germany and Samoa. They are all built with unique designs including a central dome and, usually, with nine sides to represent that this religion welcomes people of different races, nationalities and religious backgrounds.

same God and the differences relate only to where and when the revelation came. He promoted gender, racial, educational and economic equality, harmony between science and religion, and the development of a world federal system. When he died in 1957, the community made the decision to create a new way of organizing and governing themselves and of promoting their faith. They elected an international group of nine men in 1963, which created the Universal House of Justice. These people are responsible for directing spiritual and administrative affairs and are elected every five years.

This system, Bahá'ís believe, is a model for a system of world governance. The Universal House of Justice is located in Haifa, Israel, on the slopes of Mount Carmel just above the burial place of the Báb. The Shrine of Bahá'u'lláh is nearby in Acre, Israel. These two shrines are the most holy sites for Bahá'ís.

Although Bahá'ís are persecuted in some countries (according to human-rights groups, it is still not safe to practise the Bahá'í faith in Iran, and members are restricted from owning property, meeting in groups, or choosing their education), Bahá'ís are active members of the worldwide interfaith movement and work closely with the United Nations to advance human rights and environmental issues.

The Bahá'í faith is the youngest of the world's major faiths. In only 150 years, the Bahá'í message of global harmony and the oneness of all world religions is being heard around the world.

The temples are surrounded by large beautiful gardens and often fountains or pools of water. Inside, in addition to the words of the Báb and Bahá'u'lláh, you may also hear the teachings of Zoroaster, Krishna, Moses, Buddha, Jesus and Muhammad.

Rituals and Ceremonies

Bahá'ís do not have clergy or sacraments. They meet every 19 days for what is called "the 19-day feast." (There are 19 months of 19 days in the Bahá'í calendar, with "left over" days to bring the calendar in line with the 365-day Gregorian calendar.) There are three parts to their meetings: worship, time for people to talk about the community's affairs, and social time. Bahá'ís also meet for study, prayer, junior youth activities, service projects, and religious education classes for children. There are also "fireside gatherings" where people from any faith or no faith background can go to learn more about the Bahá'í faith. From these local assemblies, each country elects representatives to a nine-member national spiritual assembly to govern its affairs, coordinate, and provide a network with others. From these national assemblies, members are elected to the Universal House of Justice.

Bahá'í rituals and obligations include

- Praying and meditating each day
- Observing the holy days
- Observing the 19-day fast
- Making an effort to go on pilgrimage to the shrines of Bahá'u'lláh and the Báb
- Working to abolish racial and gender prejudice and promote unity
- Not speaking negatively about others
- Abstaining from alcohol

Rites of Passage

Weddings

Bahá'í weddings are simple and consist of the exchange of one simple vow in the presence of two witnesses: "We will all verily abide by the will of God." The wedding ceremonies are created by the couple and their families.

There are no special rites of passage or coming-of-age ceremonies for Bahá'í youth.

Golden Rule

Lay not on any soul a load that you would not wish to be laid upon you, and desire not for anyone the things you would not desire for yourself.

~ GLEANINGS FROM THE WRITINGS OF BAHÁ'U'LLÁH 66.128

Chapter 10

Multifaith World:
Only One Planet

The Role of Religions

Our faiths command us not to sit idly by amid mounting hostility and mistrust, but to make a substantial contribution to peace-building in a polarized world... The entire role of religion in the world is now at stake. Reconciliation stands little chance when narrow-minded extremists are bloodletting and sowing division in the name of our respective faiths.[1]

~ Prince El Hassan bin Talal

A Story of a Multifaith World

In his prize-winning novel, *The Life of Pi*,[2] Yann Martel takes readers on a wild lifeboat voyage with a hyena; an orangutan; a zebra with a broken leg; a Royal Bengal tiger; and Pi, a 16-year-old Indian boy. This fantastic story begins in India with Pi's search for the sacred. A day at the zoo marks his first exposure to interfaith dialogue.

"What is your son doing going to temple?" asked the priest.

"Your son was seen in church crossing himself," said the imam.

"Your son has gone Muslim," said the pandit...

Yes, it was all forcefully brought to the attention of my bemused parents. You see, they didn't know. They didn't know that I was a practicing Hindu, Christian and Muslim. Teenagers always hide a few things from their parents, isn't that so? All sixteen-year-olds have secrets, don't they? But fate decided that my parents and I and the three wise men, as I shall call them, should meet one day on the Goubert Salai seaside esplanade and that my secret should be outed... A silence fell heavily on my shoulders... "Bapu Gandhi said, 'All religions are true.' I just want to love God," I blurted out, and looked down, red in the face.

Thankfully, many people feel no embarrassment at all in sharing ideas, hopes, thoughts, stories and dreams for peace. Unlike Pi, they don't believe that they must practise one another's faith, but, like Pi, they *do* share a belief that understanding is the only way forward. Many believe that it's time for us all to join one circle and to share our personal and ancient stories. In a world that spends 12 times as much money on weapons as it does on aid to needy people, and that is having trouble getting clean water, pure air, and affordable houses for working people, we know we can no longer pretend we are separate beings. We need to work together to mend the world and to make it safe and healthy for everyone.

We rarely see news reports about religious people working together but that is not because people aren't doing it; it is because most news writers seem to believe that people want only scary news. One example of this frustrating idea was when the Canadian Broadcasting Corporation television went to the Middle East to make a documentary called "Is Peace Possible?" The interviewer talked with people in the military and politicians, but did not interview a single person from one of the many peace groups there, such as Rabbis for Peace, Religions for Peace or Women in Black.

In spite of that, there are hundreds, thousands, and millions of religious people using their energy and creativity to take a stand for peace. One example is two Ottawa high-school teens, one Jewish and one Arab, who spoke out together for peace. Another is the Arab-Jewish Women's Coalition for Peace in Edmonton, Alberta. Two by two, the women openly talk about possibilities and hope to students and others interested in peace.

Youth Assembly at the World Conference of Religions for Peace

In 2006, three-hundred religious youth leaders (ages 18–35) from around the world met at the Religions for Peace Youth Assembly in Japan. The theme was "Religious Youth for Peace: Confronting Violence and Advancing Shared Security." Youth leaders representing the world's religious traditions discussed the unique role of religious youth in preventing violence locally, regionally and globally.

To prepare for the world meeting, youth leaders held meetings in 2005 in Indonesia, the United States, Tanzania, Georgia and Lebanon. Each

Interfaith in Canada

Many religious institutions and faith communities are working hard to bring people together for discussions and for action. Two such Canadian groups are the Scarboro Missions and Faith and the Common Good. The Scarboro Missions in Toronto, Ontario, is Christian, but it is breaking ground in Canadian interfaith work, publishing interfaith materials, developing and running workshops, and working in creative ways to build understanding among communities that haven't had much to do with each other. Similarly, a multifaith organization, Faith and the Common Good brings together people across Canada to take action on issues such as poverty, the growing gap between rich and poor, and the current ecological crisis. This organization asks, "What do our religious traditions have to say about the sacredness of Earth?" and "How can our different religions work together to heal creation?" Faith and the Common Good has produced videos, posters, workshop materials and compact discs featuring music from many religious traditions.

Other local groups, such as the Edmonton Interfaith Centre for Education and Action, located in Edmonton, Alberta, holds workshops to build understanding. Panel members might talk about what they wish their neighbours knew about their faith. Women in Spirituality is a group of women from 12 different traditions in Calgary, Alberta. They hold monthly workshops to explore the feminine divine in all the traditions. Each spring, they celebrate the feminine aspect of their faiths in word, song, dance or the visual arts.

meeting analyzed violence in the region and began developing a regional inter-religious youth network.

At the world meeting, people discussed the potential for religious youth to create change through multifaith collaboration. Their objectives are to build networks of religious youth, create action plans for peaceful work after the meeting and advise the older delegates of their ideas.

Interfaith in North America

The North American Interfaith Network (NAIN) is an association of interfaith organizations and agencies in Mexico, the United States and Canada. Its mandate is to build connections and communication between groups who want to understand one another's ideas and faith, and build a more compassionate world. Its members want more understanding, co-operation and service across faiths. NAIN offers networking opportunities for people wanting information and contacts with like-minded others. The network consists of more than 50 groups. NAIN's web site and printed materials connect to a wide range of diverse groups sharing their interests. The association holds regular conferences in different parts of North America and Mexico, and these include workshops and social events.

Interfaith Worldwide

Children of Abraham is an international community of Muslim and Jewish youth who use the art of photography to explore their religious traditions, identities and to find common ground. Photographs of teens around the world in the act of praying or ritually washing, for example, show the bond shared by both groups. The web site also offers a chance for people to comment, question or honestly discuss issues in six different languages. There is also a section about role models working for Jewish-Muslim peace. Participants come from six different continents.

Women, Justice and Religion

In most religions, as in most cultures, women have not achieved equality with men. In most religions, women are kept from making decisions and are not even allowed to lead worship, although in some cases this reality is opposite to what the founders of the religions taught. This inequality shows how cultural ideas can influence more than religious ideas. Worship leaders have interpreted the holy writings in many religions to give the impression that God is a man. This preference is shown through the exclusive use of "He" when referring to God even though, in many instances, the pronoun "She" or another way of naming God altogether, such as Creator or Holy One could be used. Language has great power.

In the last century, however, people began realizing how out of balance the world had become. Women and men began to question why this imbalance had happened. They examined how we interpreted holy writings. They went back into the old stories to try to learn more about them. Equality for women does not

The World Conference of Religions for Peace

HRH Prince El Hassan bin Talal of Jordan served as moderator of The World Conference of Religions for Peace (Religions for Peace) from 1999 to 2006. His passion for peace is known around the world. He says, "It is clear that people of all religions must bridge differences and work together to ensure our survival." The mandate of Religions for Peace has members go into violent situations in such areas as Iraq, Sierra Leone, the Balkans, West Africa and the Horn of Africa. This coalition has also involved members from around the world in supporting religious communities that are working in African countries to help the 12 million who have been orphaned by HIV/AIDS. It does this work through the Hope for African Children Initiative.

Religions for Peace, which has a strong youth component and a strong women's assembly, is active on every continent and in some of the most troubled areas of the world. Its members act to help stop violence, end poverty and protect Earth. Every five years, since 1970, hundreds of religious leaders meet to plan actions for peace. Often, religious people from two sides of a conflict who can't meet at home are able to find a safe place at the conference to plan peaceful co-operation. Religions for Peace advises UNICEF and UNESCO. It is the largest international coalition of religions dedicated to promoting peace.

mean that women become like men. Instead, it means that women are respected and valued as human beings who offer a different way of looking at the world.

Dr. Zohra Husaini is a Muslim Indo-Canadian, active in the Edmonton Interfaith Centre for Education and Action. She writes,

Religions have been used and misused too long and too much to uphold the privileged position of men, and the inferior position of women in all spheres of life. It is time that the voice of true religion dissociates itself from the ignoble task of making women inferior as persons. It is time that all world religions… work for justice and equality of women which has been denied them for centuries. There is no better place to start this mission than in a free pluralistic and humanitarian country like Canada.[3]

Parliament of World Religions

A parliament of world religions was first held in Chicago in 1893 at the World's Fair. It was the first time religions from Western and Eastern spiritual traditions came together. Remembering this event, a group of religious people wanted to revive the idea of a parliament of religions and so began the Council for a Parliament of World Religions in 1988. Since then, membership has grown worldwide and the mandate has evolved to include the following: fostering understanding and co-operation between diverse peoples, communities and cultures; promoting human rights and justice; cultivating a culture of peace; and encouraging sustainable ways of living.

In 1993, the Parliament created the Declaration Toward a Global Ethic. The idea behind this document was to draw out the core values of the world's religions and to write them into a declaration that everyone could promote and encourage in their own particular traditions. The declaration is available on the Internet. In part it says:

We consider humankind our family. We must strive to be kind and generous. We must not live for ourselves alone, but should also serve others, never forgetting the children, the aged, the poor, the suffering, the disabled, the refugees and the lonely. No person should ever be considered or treated as a second-class citizen or be exploited in any way whatsoever. There should be equal partnership between men and women… We commit ourselves to a culture of non-violence, respect, justice and peace.

Neve Shalom/Wahat al Salaam

In English, *Neve Shalom/Wahat al Salaam* means "Oasis of Peace." This village, where Muslim and Christian Arabs live together in peace with Jews, is contrary to life in many parts of Israel and Palestine. Built in the 1970s on land donated by a Christian monastery, the village realized its dream for peace through the construction of homes, schools, recreation facilities, a café and shop, an international school for peace, a spiritual centre, prayer house and guest houses. In a land where violence flares too often, people can touch the reality of a peaceful coexistence. In the elementary school, children have two teachers in their classrooms – one Arab and one Jewish. The children learn about one another's religious festivals and celebrate Christian, Muslim and Jew-

Royal Institute for Interfaith Studies

In 1994, under the patronage of HRH Prince El Hassan bin Talal, the Royal Institute for Interfaith Studies was established in Amman, Jordan. This institute provides a place for study and discussion of religious issues. There has been particular attention paid to Christian-Muslim relations in Islamic society; the focus has broadened to include regional religious and cultural as well as global issues. The institute is a meeting place for established and also young scholars from Arab and non-Arab countries. It publishes information and provides networking and leadership on the world stage with other interfaith organizations.

World Peace Prayer Society

Like many Japanese people, Masahisa Goi grew up in a Buddhist-Shinto family. He was always interested in spiritual ideas, even as a child and teenager. Because he had health problems he was also interested in learning all he could about how the spirit and body affect each other and how peace affects our well-being. He was a student of music, writing, the arts, spiritual healing and yoga.

When he was 20, Goi saw the horror of World War II begin. Six years later, America dropped the first atomic bombs on Hiroshima and Nagasaki. This deepened his resolve to work for peace, health and healing – not

ish holidays. They learn one another's stories, customs and languages.

The House of Silence (*Beth Doumia/Beit as-Sakina*) is a quiet building where people from all faiths can study, celebrate, pray, listen, meditate, discuss the spiritual matter of peace, or simply enjoy silence. The School for Peace attracts people from all over the world who want to learn more about mediation and peacemaking. Volunteers from around the world work at the Oasis to become part of a community dedicated to peace.

In 2006, while the bombs were flying from Lebanon into Israel and vice versa, 22-year-old Ranin Boulos was running a peace camp for Palestinian children from refugee camps in Jenin, Tulkarm and Yaabad. Although the geographic distance is not great between the Oasis of Peace and these communities, it takes many hours to travel past army checkpoints, have identity papers checked and stand in humiliating lineups. The children had never been inside Israel before; the only Jews they had ever met were soldiers.

Ranin, with help from other young adults, teens and children, ran the camp for a week. She was born and raised at Neve Shalom/Wahat al Salaam and now attends university in London, England.

only within himself, his family and friends but also in his country and, ultimately, the world. Goi undertook a rigorous spiritual training and, at age 33, attained enlightenment. He then became a spiritual counsellor and offered himself to help heal a devastated nation. In 1955, he began the World Peace Prayer Society. The message of the society was then – and is still today – simple: may peace prevail on Earth. The Peace Pole Project is one method the society uses to spread this message. A peace pole is a monument (made from wood or granite usually) that has painted, etched or carved the society's message and prayer on each of its sides, usually in different languages. From Japan, the idea of planting a peace pole has spread to 180 countries, and it is estimated that today there are more than 200,000 peace poles around the world.

Among the places peace poles have been planted are Yellowknife, Northwest Territories, and the co-operative village Neve Shalom/Wahat al Salaam in Israel. It is a welcome and encouraging sign to be out for a walk and come across a peace pole in a park or garden, but the planting of them is

International Peace Prayer[4]

This prayer is alternately attributed to Jains, Christians and Hindus.

Lead me from death to life
from falsehood to truth
lead me from despair to hope
from fear to trust
lead me from hate to love
from war to peace
let peace fill our hearts
our world, our universe.

A Women's Interfaith Journey

also significant. There are no set rules for how to plant a peace pole; people can be as creative as they like. People from different backgrounds and beliefs come together – teens, children and elders – thinking about and praying for one single hope, that peace prevail on Earth. Some people hold simple ceremonies; others make an elaborate celebration with prayers sung and danced and feasts shared.

Traditionally, the work of inter-religious dialogue has been organized by men. In the late 1990s, the Henry Martyn Institute (HMI) in India and the United Church of Canada wanted to take a new step in interfaith dialogue. HMI is an international centre for research, interfaith relations, and reconciliation. It is dedicated to studying and teaching about Islam and to promoting inter-faith dialogue. The United Church is a liberal Canadian church, the union of three Christian denominations – Presbyterian, Congregationalist, and Methodist. The two bodies decided to experiment with the question: What would happen if women engaged in interfaith dialogue? What would they do? Would it be different from or the same as what men do?

The first thing HMI and the United Church decided was to send women on a journey, rather than ask them to meet in a conference centre or

UN Charter of Rights and Freedoms

Article 18 of the United Nations Charter of Rights and Freedoms states that: Everyone has the right to freedom of thought, conscience and religion; this right includes freedom to change his or her religion or belief, and freedom, either alone or in community with others and in public or private, to manifest his or her religion or belief in teaching, practice, worship and observance.

institute. They decided to invite four Canadians and four Indian women to try out the idea. Four Canadians – one Cree (Aboriginal) Elder, one Muslim, one Hindu, and one Christian woman – travelled to India to meet their counterparts and the facilitator. The nine women travelled together for nearly a month, visiting women's groups that work for peace in conflict zones and slums, and groups working against spousal abuse and for literacy. Every day, the nine women sat in a sharing circle. The circle, which Cree Elder Myra Laramee taught them, kept the women focused and centred.

The women did not worry about the rules of religion, dogmas or theology. They shared their sacred lives with each other. They didn't talk about interfaith or get into debates – they connected as humans concerned with protecting Earth, cherishing the next generation, raising families and honouring one another as friends. They learned from one another and also had time for self-reflection. They made space for discussion, prayer, art, music, laughter, tears and fun – in short, they lived together.

Some months after their return, the group of nine met again in Canada and travelled in two provinces. They listened to Canadian women involved in healing, anti-poverty, literacy, race relations and immigration.

Three more journeys organized by HMI have taken place between different tribal groups in northern India, between Kenyan and Indian women, and between Sri Lankan and Indian women. In Canada, United Church women brought together four groups of Aboriginal and non Aboriginal women.

Child Honouring

Raffi Cavoukian has devoted his life to children. As a singer, he is loved by children around the world. One of his most famous songs, "Baby Beluga," is a love song about an endangered animal. It was the cancers found in beluga whales in the St. Lawrence River that turned Raffi's attention from entertaining children to learning as much as he could about the planet that children are inheriting. What he discovered alarmed him. Adults, he decided, need to act now to create a world fit for children

and thus for all of us. Increasingly his new song titles began to reflect this message, and his attention became more focused on how to turn this world around. Raffi wrote *A Covenant for Honouring Children* as another way of calling attention to the youngest citizens and their need for a safe and healthy planet. Working with religious leaders, child psychiatrists, educators and policy makers, Raffi is making child honouring a powerful force for change in the world.

In the anthology *Child Honoring: How to Turn this World Around,* theologian Heather Eaton writes, "While each religion has distinct contributions, common ground is necessary if we are to address the current global crises. It is possible to appreciate each religious tradition as offering specific insights and teachings within what Thomas Berry calls a tapestry of revelations... [We cannot] think of economics, psychology, sciences and even religion without considering the centrality of

Conclusion

the Earth. This is a new – and ancient – religious awakening!"[5]

In the foreword to this book, the Dalai Lama says,

> Many of the world's problems and conflicts arise because we have lost sight of the basic humanity that binds us all together as a human family. We tend to forget that despite the diversity of race, religion, ideology and so forth people are equal in the basic wish for peace and happiness. In this, children have much to teach adults.[6]

One of the Ten Commandments known to Jewish, Christian and Muslim people is "Honour your mother and father." A commitment by people of all religions (or no religion) to honour children could give a new starting point for everyone; every family on Earth wants a safe and healthy home for their little ones.

The following Hindu tale gives us a metaphor for how sharing our ideas can give us the big picture. A group of people wanted to know what an elephant was like. They were blind, but they thought that if they got the creature to stand still and used their hands to feel it gently, they could figure it out. An obliging elephant stood still while the people felt all over it. One person felt its trunk and declared that an elephant was like a tree – tall, thick, with a rough bark. Another felt the tail and declared that an elephant is like a stiff rope with wiry things stuck into the end. A third person carefully felt an ear, running his fingers around the edge and across the centre. He declared that an elephant is like a canvas sail on a boat, smooth and firm. Everyone had a different idea of what an elephant is like.

Every day, the network of outward-facing religions becomes bigger, stronger and more inventive. This is the hope of seeing the big picture. We do not need to give up who we are or what we believe. We do not need to convince others that we have the only one right answer. The task ahead is to celebrate our diversity, learn from each other and find creative ways to work together to heal the world. I think that we all have an idea of the sacred, but like the people in the tale we cannot see the big picture. I believe that the religions, like the people with the elephant, need to share their impressions and discoveries. We have much wisdom to share.

Notes

[1] From "Confronting Violence and Advancing Shared Security." Address of HRH Prince El Hassan bin Talal at the Opening Ceremony of Assembly of the World Conference of Religions for Peace, Kyoto, Japan, August 26, 2006.

[2] Yann Martel, *The Life of Pi* (Toronto: Vintage Canada, 2001), 71, 76.

[3] Reinhold Boehm and Zohra Husaini, eds., *In the Name of Religion: Impact of Fundamentalism on the Status of Women* (Edmonton, AB: Indo-Canadian Women's Association, 1994) 111–112.

[4] From: http://www.liturgy.co.nz/html/byheartcurrent.html

[5] Raffi Cavoukian and Sharna Olfman, eds., *Child Honouring: How to Turn this World Around* (Westport, CT: Praeger Press, 2006), 78–79.

[6] Ibid, x.

Appendix 1

More Traditions

Agnostic This word was invented by Thomas Huxley, a scientist. It comes from the Greek *a* ("without") and *gnosis* ("knowledge"). An agnostic is someone who is skeptical about the existence of God.

Atheist Someone who denies the existence of God. (The opposite of a theist.)

Confucianism This religion or way of life was founded by K'ung Fu Tzu (551 – 479 BCE) in China. He wrote and taught about moral behaviour and ethics, and was critical of politicians of the day. This religion has existed side by side with Taoism and Buddhism. Followers live mostly in China, Asia and North America.

Jainism Founded by Vardhamana, or "The Great Hero" (born 599 BCE), in India. Jains are so committed to non-violence that they are vegetarians. The religion contains other beliefs that are similar to those in Buddhism and Hinduism.

Jehovah's Witnesses Charles Russell, an American, began this offshoot of Christianity in the 1800s. Jehovah's Witnesses understand the Bible literally. They go door-to-door and stand on street corners to try to convert people to their beliefs. One of the beliefs they will die for is that it is wrong to accept blood transfusions.

Mormons Members of the Church of Jesus Christ of Latter-day Saints. This church began in 1823 in the United States when Joseph Smith was visited by an angel named Moroni. The angel revealed the Book of Mormon, which is understood as a history, a guide to salvation and new revelations about Jesus. Mormons often live in communities apart from other people. Many live in state of Utah.

Rastafarianism An offshoot of Coptic (African) Christianity. Emperor Haile Selassie of Ethiopia is considered a prophet in modern times. The movement became especially popular in Jamaica, due to the work of musician Bob Marley.

Sai Baba Swami Sai Baba is considered a living god by his followers. Born in India in 1926, he is believed to perform miracles of healing. His followers have built hospitals, and work for the poor in Asia.

Shinto *Shinto* means "the way of the gods," and began in Japan around 1000 BCE. Shintoism combines Confucianism and Buddhism to help shape Japanese culture and ways of life. Amaterasu, the Sun Goddess, and the spirits in nature are important in Shinto spirituality. Shinto priests beat large drums to wake up the spirits present in nature. Shinto rituals are often used with Buddhist traditions; in Japan most weddings are Shinto ceremonies, but most funerals are Buddhist ceremonies.

Taoism *Tao* means "the Way" (*taoism* is pronounced DOW-ism). It was started in China by Lao Tzu about 500 BCE. Lao Tzu taught people to care for their health and well-being through chanting, meditation and exercise. He wrote a book called *Tao Te Ching*, which means "the Way and Its Power." Tai chi comes from the Taoist tradition, and the yin yang symbol represents balance.

Unitarianism Some Unitarians consider themselves Christians; others do not. They believe in the oneness of God and understand Jesus as a great teacher. The Unitarian movement began in the 1500s during the Protestant Reformation in Europe. Members have always emphasized reason and science. They are usually involved in working for human rights.

Zoroastrianism Around 1500 BCE, Zoroaster (or Zarathustra) of Persia (today Iran) taught people about his belief that there was one God. He taught that if you are good you will go to heaven, and if you are bad you will go to hell when you die. At the end of time, he said, people's spirits would be reunited with their bodies and they would live forever. Most *parsis* (which translates literally as "Persians," but means follower of Zoroaster) live in India today. Fire is sacred to them because it purifies.

Appendix 2

A Word about Cults

Sometimes people who do not have a clear understanding of religion or spirituality can get caught in a cult that is unhealthy and even dangerous. There have been horrible examples of cults in modern times, where whole groups of women, children, and men have killed themselves by suicide, believing that they were being threatened or believing that they'd go straight to heaven because some leader told them so. Cult members are always looking for recruits.

Stories about young people enticed by cult members appear from time to time in the news. In 2006, a Canadian teenager was accused of helping to murder her own family members after becoming involved in a cult. In the United States, two dramatic stories of cult deaths have actually been made into films.

Jim Jones started the Peoples' Temple in the 1970s. He convinced about 1,000 Americans that they should sell everything and move to a village he got them to build in Guyana, South America. They believed they were going to paradise. He named the village Jonestown. In 1978, he ordered the murder and suicide of everyone there; only a few people survived. Another disaster took place in 1993 near Waco, Texas, when rumours about child sexual abuse, polygamy, and weapons began circulating. When federal agents went to investigate, both agents and cult members were killed. After a siege lasting almost two months, federal agents surrounded the compound and 88 children and adults died in a horrible fire, including the leader of the group, David Koresh. Several documentary films and books have explored the beliefs of the people and what led up to their deaths.

What Is a Cult?

How do you know if you are being invited to join a religion or a cult that could get you in trouble? What questions can you ask? What clues should you look for?

Cults can look like religions from the outside, with symbols, leaders, special dress codes and music. They will also have some characteristics that you need to look at carefully.

1) They want you all to themselves.
2) They will not want you to tell your family much about them.
3) They will "love" you instantly.
4) They want your money but won't necessarily tell you what they do with it.
5) They work best with people who are lonely, tired, and do not have good self-esteem.
6) They may use language like "us" and "them" and encourage you to think you are different from your friends or family (and only like them).
7) They may want everyone in the group to think and feel the same, rather than as individuals.
8) They may ask you to prove your loyalty to the leader or to the group.
9) They may ask you to perform a physical or psychological ritual that makes you feel creepy.
10) They don't want you to ask too many questions.

Common sense, strong self-esteem, and asking good questions are your best protection against getting caught in a cult. If you want to learn more about cults, check out websites or books written by people who have escaped from cults. Teachers of world religion classes or school counsellors could also help you become informed. If the religious group you are wondering about is safe, people there will welcome your questions and independent investigations about them.

Appendix 3

Two Generations Talk about Religion and Peace

Mira D'Souza

Mira D'Souza lives in Milton, near Boston, Massachussetts, and is in grade 12. She has lived in Hyderabad, India, where she was exposed to interfaith relationships from an early age; and in Canada.

Diane D'Souza, her mother, is an American writer, artist and peacemaker, who co-founded a series of Women's Interfaith Journeys for Peace. Here, Mira and Diane each reflect on their own experiences.

I was born in Hyderabad, India, a city known for its rich history and beautiful pearls, into a family of Indian, Swiss and English ethnicities. I took this diversity for granted, especially since I lived on the campus of an international research and study institute, and developed lasting friendships with people of all different nationalities and religious backgrounds. As a child, I was not aware of any boundaries that divide people on the basis of religion.

For my primary education, I went to a school that had a diverse population, and therefore my time in and outside of school was spent with friends of different faiths. On Diwali (the Hindu festival of lights), I would celebrate with my friends, watching colourful firecrackers light up the sky. During Ramadan, I would visit family friends to break

their day of fasting with them, taking pleasure in the rich flavour of haleem (which is a porridge made with wheat and lamb). If I had a sleepover, my friends would attend mass with my family on Sunday mornings and sing along with the church choir. Every new experience with a different religion catalyzed my curiosity about how people expressed their faith.

These experiences, more than anything, shaped my fundamental attitude towards people and faith traditions. They led me to participate in discussions, on committees and in groups that bring people together across faiths and racial backgrounds. And they led me to decide that, in college, I want to pursue international business, with a focus on socially responsible business. (Two years ago, I moved to the United States, and I am now in the process of applying to different colleges.)

I believe that it is important for people of various religions to work together, because there is so much we can learn from each other. Many religions have sets of rules that may seem strange to others. For example, Jains do not believe in killing any living being, and so, many wear masks to prevent them from breathing in stray organisms. Without religious tolerance, there would be misunderstandings and narrow-mindedness. Speaking from my experiences, I believe that the best way to promote interfaith understanding is to bring together children of various religions so that they form close bonds with each other before religious barriers drive them apart.

Religion is sometimes overlooked by teens. After all, it is hard to associate ancient religious tales with the struggles that today's youth face. I value religion not because of these stories but rather because of the morals that you learn from them. I hope teens will keep themselves open to both the differences and the similarities between faiths. I believe this is key to greater insight and understanding.

Diane D'Souza

Religion and peace are big words. I'll address them one at a time before bringing them together. Peace isn't what I used to think it was. As a teenager, I might have described it as people and countries all getting along — no wars, no fear of bombs or air-raids, everyone being friends.

That's not a bad idea, but I think it's incomplete. The fact is, even friends sometimes disagree, make mistakes, or hurt each other. Peace doesn't mean the absence of times of conflict or pain. It suggests ways to handle such challenges when they do happen. It helps us think: How do I find my way through this difficult place? How do I act in a way that respects both me and the other person or people in this relationship?

I'm also learning that peace sometimes means separation. There are times when being friends might just not be possible — for people or countries. When someone or something is hurting us, we may need to get distance in order to survive or gain strength or clarity. It reminds me of when a vine wraps itself around the branches of a bush or tree. Some vines cling so tightly that they start to kill the other plant. The two cannot live that close together if both are to survive. I believe peace is about the opportunity for all of us

to live abundantly. Sometimes living abundantly means struggle, fighting for change, or even separation. Only when we are strong enough are we able to return to build a new relationship in a healthy way.

The way I think of peace now is rather like a guiding star. Sailors used to use the stars to chart their travel before there were computers or radar. The positions of the stars revealed directions, like the North Star or the sun (our closest star). Peace for me is a bit like those stars. It guides our direction; it's not a destination we ever reach. When I'm in a situation which is challenging, I can ask: Do my actions, do the other person's actions guide us in the direction of peace? Do they help bring greater life for all?

Religion at its best is also about greater life. I've met some people who say it has saved their lives, helping them find safety and comfort in times of terrible trouble. It has brought them healing. I know others whose lives have changed positively because people — motivated by religious beliefs — have reached out and helped them. One example is a friend of mine who went to school and became a social worker, a leader in her community. She says it would never have happened if it weren't for a priest who saw a little girl too poor to attend school, and made sure there was a place for her. He was encouraging when others weren't and gave her the help she needed to succeed.

To my mind, one of the best things about a religion is often the community of people it brings together. When I moved into a new town a couple of years ago, I started going to a church. People were glad to see me and I started to develop friendships. I enjoyed having people to talk and listen to, to care about and who cared about me. I also liked how this community of friends cared about our town — how we regularly brought cans and boxes of food to give to the food pantry, where families went when they needed groceries but were short on money, or how people would rally together, contributing time or money to help a project at a school or at a hospice, which gives assistance to people who are dying. A lot of good can happen in the world when people come together and decide to do something positive. A religious community can bring greater light into our world that way.

But religion can also increase arrogance, hatred, misunderstanding and destruction. I've seen religion be used to encourage people to hate others or to identify an enemy to hate. I've heard people pray for the destruction of their enemies, confident that God rewards efforts to kill "the bad guys." History shows us that religion helped Europeans believe that God gave them the land we now know as

North America, even though others already lived there. Religion has helped us enslave and colonize people, and demean those who are different from ourselves. We've even drawn boundaries within religions, dividing people because we believe our way of being religious is right and the others is wrong. Religion has also encouraged us to place ourselves above Earth and its other creatures, leading us to carelessly damage our beautiful planet.

Like many things, then, religion brings both good and bad into the world. It can be a resource for us as we struggle to increase peace. It can also cause us to belittle, disrespect and harm others. We need to keep our eyes open and our minds active when we think of religion as a resource for positive change.

Our world needs more peace, and it is easy to feel discouraged about our progress. We look at people starting wars or refusing to end them; at companies making arms and tanks and submarines; at people not having enough to eat or losing their homes or getting sick; at violence taking place in families; at our poor Earth struggling with overdevelopment, pollution and people refusing responsibility for the mess they make. What I've learned is that, while I may keep my eye on these sad and terrible truths, I also need to seek out the places where people are making positive steps to increase peace. These are the people who give me hope and the energy to keep going. I'm not talking about the big-name kind of peacemakers, like Mahatma Gandhi, Rosa Parks or Nelson Mandela, even though they may inspire us. I'm talking about the ordinary everyday kind of peacemakers. Like kids who speak up in school when someone is being teased, and the women who weekly come together as part of the worldwide movement Women in Black to protest violence and wars. The person who slows down their car so another can enter the traffic ahead of them, and widows whose husbands died in the collapse of the World Trade Center, who reach out to help war widows in Afghanistan. Children who collect money to help build schools for others who don't have them, and people who donate blood so that the injured or sick can have a chance to get well. Peace takes many shapes, but there is always an opportunity to choose to increase it in our own homes, schools, work places and communities. We don't have to wait for our political leaders to take the lead. We can be creative actors ourselves. Building peace is a challenging lesson we all need to get better at — wherever and whoever we are.

Appendix 4

For Further Exploration

Web sites*

Web sites of organizations or movements referred to in this book are listed below.

Child Honouring: www.raffinews.com

Children of Abraham: www.children-of-abraham.org

Neve Shalom/Wahat al Salaam (Oasis of Peace): www.nswas.org

North American Interfaith Network (NAIN): www.nain.org

PeaceJam International: www.peacejam.org

World Peace Prayer Society: www.worldpeace.org/minute_of_silence.html. Also see www.worldpeace.org/peacepoles.html

* Please note: these websites and those listed in the Chapter Resources were current at the time of publication.

Additional Resources

The following resources provide opportunities to further explore themes in the book, including myths and legends, spirituality, multifaith work, and youth leadership.

The Power of Myth, by Joseph Campbell, is a series of books, videos and DVDs. Explore Campbell's work at: www.jcf.org.

What the Bleep Do We Know!? DVD, directed by William Arntz (Capri Films, 2004). Please see: www.whatthebleep.com

One: The Movie. DVD, directed by Ward Powers (Circle of Bliss Productions, 2006). Please see: www.onethemovie.org

Ontario Consultants on Religious Tolerance has three objectives: to promote religious tolerance and freedom, to objectively describe religious faiths in all their diversity, and to objectively describe controversial topics from all points of view. Please see: www.religioustolerance.org/

The Multifaith Calendar is created by a committee in Port Moody, British Columbia. It is a full-colour art calendar with the holy days of 13 faith groups marked and briefly explained. You may visit the Multifaith Society website at www.multifaithaction. org. Calendars may be ordered from several places including: Edmonton Interfaith Centre, 11148 – 84 Avenue, Edmonton, Alberta T6G OV8 Canada.
(phone: 780 413-6159) and CoNexus Press, PO Box 39218, Solon, Ohio 44139 USA (phone toll free: 1-877-784-7779).

Leaders Today is dedicated to helping young people realize their fullest potential through leadership education and development, using an innovative, youth-inspired curriculum. Canadians Marc and Craig Kielburger started Leaders Today with the vision to empower youth to become socially involved. This is not an interfaith movement, but youth who follow any religion or no religion could find it a great group to connect with because its ethics are common. Please see: www.leaderstoday.com

Chapter Resources

For all chapters

Beversluis, Joel, ed. *Sourcebook of the World's Religions: An Interfaith Guide to Religion and Spirituality.* Novato, CA: New World Library, 2000.

Bowker, John, ed. *Concise Dictionary of World Religions.* Oxford: Oxford University Press, 2000.

Gellman, Marc, and Thomas Hartman. *Religion for Dummies: A Reference for the Rest of Us!* Indianapolis: Indian Wiley Publishing Inc., 2002.

Glossop, Jennifer. *The Kids Book of World Religions.* Toronto: Kids Can Press, 2003.

Neusner, Jacob, ed. *World Religions in America: An Introduction.* Louisville: Westminster John Knox Press, 2000.

Nielsen, Niels C., ed. *Religions of the World.* 3rd ed. New York: St. Martin's Press, 1993.

Smith, Jonathan Z., et al., eds. *The HarperCollins Dictionary of Religion.* HarperSanFrancisco, 1995.

Chapter 1:
In the Beginning… The Goddess Tradition

Brooke, Elisabeth. *Medicine Women: A Pictorial History of Women Healers.* Wheaton, OH: Quest Books, 1997.

Chaline, Eric. *The Book of Gods and Goddesses: A Visual Directory of Ancient and Modern Deities.* New York: HarperCollins, 2004.

Milne, Courtney, and Sherrill Miller. *Visions of the Goddess.* Toronto: Penguin, 1998.

Muten, Burleigh, and Rebecca Guay. *Goddesses: A World of Myth and Magic.* Cambridge: Barefoot Books, 2003.

Oestre/Easter: www.aznewage.com/easter.htm

Rabinovitch, Shelley, and James Lewis. *The Encyclopedia of Modern Witchcraft and Neo-Paganism.* New York: Citadel Press, 2002.

Read, Donna, and Starhawk. *Signs Out of Time: The Story of Archaeologist Marija Gimbutas*, DVD. San Francisco, CA: Belili Productions, 2003. See also: www. gimbutas.org

Read, Donna. *Goddess Remembered.* VHS. Montreal: Studio D, National Film Board of Canada, 1989. See also: *The Burning Times* and *Full Circle* in this Women and Spirituality series.

Stewart, Maureen, and Graeme Base. *Creation Stories.* Toronto: Stoddart Publishing, 1989.

Wells, Rosalie. *Goddess Mythology, Women's Spirituality, and Ecofeminism.* Athabasca, AB: Athabasca University, 2001.

Chapter 2: Aboriginal Spirituality

Aboriginal: www.webwinds.com/yupanqui/apachesunrise.htm

Asanee Watchew Iskwiw: Mountain Woman. *Teachings.* Self-published, 2000.

Citizens for Public Justice (brochure), Toronto.

Martin, Joel W. *The Land Looks After Us: A History of Native American Religion.* New York: Oxford University Press, 2001.

Native American Spirituality. VHS, from the *Religions of the World* series (Grade 9 and up), Schlessinger Media, 1998.

Pogue, Carolyn. *Seasons of Peace: Teachers' Resource.* Courtenay, BC: Connections Publishing, 2007.

Six Nations: www.sixnations.buffnet.net/Great_Law_of_Peace

Solomon, Arthur. *Songs of the People: Teachings on the Natural Way.* Toronto: New Canada Publications, 1990.

Vision Quest: www.history.cbc.ca/history

Zimmerman, Larry J. *Native North America.* Toronto: Little, Brown and Company, 1996.

Chapter 3: Hinduism

Gopal, Ramya. "Coming of Age: How my Faith Honors the Mothers of Tomorrow." *Hinduism Today.* October-December 2004. Please see: www.hinduismtoday.com

Hinduism: www.hinduism.about.com/od/basics

Hinduism: www.hinduism.iskcon.com/tradition/1105.htm

Human Rights Watch, "Caste Violence in India," www.hrw.org/reports/1999/india

M.K.Gandhi Institute for Nonviolence, 650 East Parkway South, Memphis, Tennessee 38104 USA. Please see: www.gandhiinstitute.org

Maharishi Mahesh Yogi: www.tm.org

Prayer: www.indianchild.com/hindu_prayers.htm

Viswanathan, Edakkandiyil. *Am I a Hindu? The Hinduism Primer.* San Francisco: Halo Books, 1992.

Additional note: *Gandhi,* the film starring Ben Kingsley, won nine Oscars. It is available on DVD. Also, Indo-Canadian filmmaker Deepa Mehta has made three films exploring controversial Hindu themes. *Water,* which is about child brides and widowhood, was released in 2005.

Chapter 4: Judaism

Brief History of the Jews: www.bbc.co.uk/religion/religions/judaism/history/history5.shtml (Note: no women are interviewed in this film and no feminine perspective is presented.)

Mooney, Clint, ed. *Bearing Faithful Witness.* Toronto:United Church of Canada, 2003.

Rabbi Sandy Eisenberg Sasso: www.skylightpaths.com. See also www.beliefnet.com

Schlessinger Media. *Judaism.* Religions of the World series, 1998.

Witty, Rachel J. *A Vocabulary of Jewish Tradition.* Calgary: Letter Perfect, 1985.

Yad Vashem Holocaust Memorial, Israel: www.yad-vashem.org.il/exhibitions

Chapter 5: Buddhism

Bodian, Stephan. *Meditation for Dummies.* Foster City, CA: IDG Books Worldwide Inc, 1999.

Buddhism: www.buddhism. About.com/library/weekly/aa032103a.htm

Buddhism: www.buddhistchannel.tv/index

Hanh, Thich Nhat. *Peace is Every Step: The Path of Mindfulness in Everyday Life.* New York: Bantam Books, 1992.

Thompson, Mel. *Buddhism.* Vancouver: Whitecap Books, 2004.

Chapter 6: Christianity

Martin Luther King, Jr.: www.thekingcenter.org/

Poortvliet, Rien, and Hans Bouma. *He was One of Us: The Life of Jesus of Nazareth.* New York: Doubleday and Company, 1986.

Scarboro United Church, *Communion liturgy.* September bulletin, 2006.

Zundel, Veronica, compiler. *Christian Classics.* Grand Rapids, MI: William B. Eerdmans Publishing Company, 1985.

Chapter 7: Islam

Ebadi, Shirin. *Iran Awakening: From Prison to Peace Prize.* Toronto: Alfred A. Knopf Canada, 2006.

Hamdon, Karen, telephone interview with the author, August 22, 2006.

Islam: www.bbc.co.uk/worldservice/people/features/world_religions/islam_life. html

Islam: www.cbc.ca/news/background/islam

Mernissi, Fatima. *Dreams of Trespass: Tales of a Harem Girlhood.* Toronto: Addison-Wesley Publishing, 1994.

Islam: Empire of Faith, VHS. Directed by Karpo Acimovic-Godina. Public Broadcast Service, 1995. See also: www.pbs.org

"That We May Know Each Other: United Church-Muslim Relations Today." (study document) Toronto: United Church of Canada, 2004. Please see: www.united-church.ca/twmkeo/pdf/report.pdf

Chapter 8: Sikhism

Penney, Sue. *Sikhism: Discovering Religions.* Austin, TX: Raintree Steck-Vaughn Publishers, 1997.

Sikhism: www.sikhnet.com

Sikhism: www.sikhs.org/trans17.htm

Chapter 9: Bahá'í Faith

Bahá'í World Centre, Office of Public Information. *The Bahá'ís.* Haifi, Israel: Bahá'í International Community, 2005.

Bahá'í: www.religioustolerance.org/bahai1.htm

Bahá'í: www.bci.org/scotland/quest/temples.htm

Official Bahá'í Web site: www.bahai.org

Chapter 10: Multifaith World: Only One Planet

Boehm, Reinhold, and Zohra Husaini, eds. *In the Name of Religion: Impact of Fundamentalism on the Status of Women.* Edmonton, AB: Indo-Canadian Women's Association, 1994.

Cavoukian, Raffi, and Sharna Olfman, eds. *Child Honouring: How to Turn this World Around.* Westport, CT: Praeger Press, 2006.

"Confronting Violence and Advancing Shared Security." Address of HRH Prince El Hassan bin Talal at the Opening Ceremony of Assembly of the World Conference of Religions for Peace, Kyoto, Japan, August 26, 2006.

Martel, Yann. *The Life of Pi.* Toronto: Vintage Canada, 2001.

Prayer: www.liturgy.co.nz/html/byheartcurrent.html

Index

Credits

p. 12: © Selin Ogeturek/iStock
p. 13: © Loon Yik Herng/iStock (Dandilion)
p. 14: © Chris Schmidt/iStock
p. 15: © James Steidl/iStock
p. 16: © Chris Schmidt/iStock
p. 18: © Lena Gronwall/iStock
p. 19: © Supterstock/m a X x images;
© Carolina K. Smith, M.D./iStock
p. 20: © Archivo Iconografico, S.A./CORBIS;
© Feng Yu/iStock
p. 21: © Burstein Collection/CORBIS;
© iStock
p. 22: © Newberry Library/m a X x images
(Yggdrasil Tree); adapted from
© Richard Schmidt-Zuper (hand),
© Jan Rysavy (globe)
p. 23: © Paige Foster/iStock
p. 24: © Marina Yakutsenya/iStock (Sedna);
© Andy Rain/epa/CORBIS
p. 26: © Andrew Gentry/iStock (leaves);
© iStock (icicles);
© Denise Torres/iStock (lilac);
© Olga Langerova/iStock (berries)
p. 32: © Marilyn Angel Wynn/Nativestock.com;
© Nancy Nehring/iStock
p. 33: © Marilyn Angel Wynn/Nativestock.com;
p. 34: © Marilyn Angel Wynn/Nativestock.com
p. 35: © Arthur Matkovskyy/iStock;
© Marilyn Angel Wynn/Nativestock.com
p. 36: © Marilyn Angel Wynn/Nativestock.com
p. 37: © John Woodstock/iStock;
© Marilyn Angel Wynn/Nativestock.com
p. 39: © Paul Senysnyn/iStock;
© Marilyn Angel Wynn/Nativestock.com
p. 40: public domain
p. 41: © Marilyn Angel Wynn/Nativestock.com
p. 50: © iStock
p. 51: © Ann Triling/iStock;
© Michal Rozanski/ iStock
p. 52: public domain;
© Hector Joseph Luman/iStock
p. 53: © iStock; Flemming Pless/iStock
p. 54: © Flemming Pless/iStock;
© Ashwin Kharidehal/iStock
p. 55: © Bettmann/CORBIS (Gandhi);
public domain
p. 56: © Lise Gagne/iStock
p. 57: ©Zoubin Zarin/iStock;
© Anna Cegllinska/iStock
p. 58: © iStcok
p. 64: © Steven Allan/iStock (both images)
p. 65: © Peter Spiro/iStock;
© Howard Sandler/iStock
p. 66: © James Steidle/iStock;
© Lisa F. Young/iStock; © iStock
p. 67: © Margaret Kyle, Wood Lake
Publishing Inc.

p. 68: © Anssi ruuska/iStock
p. 69: © Sébastien Désarmaux/Godong/
CORBIS
p. 71: © 2004 Yad Vashem The Holocaust
Martyrs' and Heroes' Rememberence
Authority. www.yadvashem.org;
© istock (Anne Frank)
p. 72: © Claudia Dewald/iStock
p. 73: © Odelia Cohen/iStock;
© iStock;
© Nancy Louie/iStock
p. 74: © Rose Eichenbaum/CORBIS
p. 80: © istock (Buddha statue);
© Christine Gonsalves/iStock
p. 81: © Allan Brown/iStock;
© Jupiterimages/photos.com
p. 82: © Marc Dietrich/iStock;
© Rebecca Ames/iStock;
© Heidi Priesnitz/iStock
p. 83: © istock
p. 84: © Tom Werner/iStock;
© Carrie Keill/iStock
p. 85: © Uri Ar/iStock;
© Micha Rosenwirth/iStock
p. 86: ©Imre Cikajlo/iStock;
puplic domain (Dalai Lama)
p. 88: © Daniel Baumgartner/iStock;
© istock
p. 89: © Leonard de Salva/CORBIS;
© Lisa. F. Young/iStock
p. 90: © Huamg Xiang/iStock;
p. 96: © Corey Sundahl/iStock;
© Leslie Banks/iStock
p. 97: © David Dea/iStock
p. 98: © Tari Faris/iStock;
© Jean Schweitzer/iStock;
p. 99: © Iacobescu Alexandru/iStock;
© istock (empty cross);
© Kim Freitas/iStock
p. 100: public domain (M.L.King);
© Magdalena Kucova/iStock;
© Glenda Powers/iStock
p. 101: © Aldo Murillo/iStock
p. 102: © Leonardo de Salva/CORBIS
p. 103: public domain;
© Phillipe Lissac/Godong/CORBIS;
public domain (Martin Luther)
p. 104: © iStock
p. 105: public domain; © Eric Hood/iStock
p. 106: © Terry Healy/iStock
p. 114: public domain
p. 115: public domain
p. 116: © photos.com; © Joe Brandt/iStock;
© NIcholas Belton/iStock;
© Aman Khan/iStock
p. 117: © Swayasu Tsuji/iStock;
© Kazuyoshi Nomachi/CORBIS

p. 118: © Canadian Islamic Centre
www.muslim-canada.org; © CORBIS
p. 119: © Canadian Islamic Centre
www.muslim-canada.org;
© Steve Allen/Brand X/CORBIS
p. 120: © Bettmann/CORBIS
p. 121: © Kaye Kerr/iStock
p. 122: © Murat Sen/iStock
p. 130: © Loic Bernard/iStock
p. 131: © Estate of Amolak Singh. Used by
permission of Kiranpal Singh
p. 132: © Dinodia/m a X x images
p. 133: © iStock
p. 134: © Estate of Amolak Singh. Used by
permission of Kiranpal Singh (Sikh Gurus)
p. 135 © Catherine Jones/iStock;
© Estate of Amolak Singh. Used by
permission of Kiranpal Singh (Sikh Gurus)
p. 137: © Jennifer Leigh Sauer/Photonica/
gettyimages
p. 138: © Umbar Shakir/iStock;
© Tim Page/CORBIS
p. 146: © Erik Lam/iStock
p. 149: public domain
p. 151: public domain
p. 152: © Steve Adamson/iStock
p. 153: © Steve Geer/iStock
p. 154: © Tony Ashby/Striger/AFP/
gettyimages
p. 157: © Jason Benedict/iStock (globe)
p. 158: © iStock
p. 159: © Andrea Gingerich/iStock;
© Elena Elisseeva/iStock
p. 160: © David Mesarch/iStock
p. 161: © Don Bayley/iStock
p. 164: public domain
p. 165: © Stan Rohrer/iStock
p. 166: © Sthpen Rees/iStock;
adapted from iStock
p. 167: © iStock
p. 168: © Michael Kemter/iStock;
© Jay and Varina Patel/iStock
p. 170: © Norbert Zeller/iStock
p. 171: © Gautier Willaume/iStock;
© iStock
p. 175: © iStock
p. 176: © iStock
p. 177: © Achim Prill/iStock
p. 178: © Pavel Losevsky/iStock

Green and Golden Rules artwork:
© Verena Velten;
© Eva Serrabassa/iStock (hand);
© Bob Randall/iStock (circle of hands);
© Katsiaryna Trapeznikava/iStock (vines)

photos on front and back cover:
© iStock; photos.com; gettyimages.com

Interfaith and Youth Resources from Wood Lake Publishing

Youth Spirit
Program Ideas for Youth Groups
Compiled by Cheryl Perry
978-1-55145-247-0

Youth Spirit
More Program Ideas for Youth Groups
Compiled by Cheryl Perry
978-1-55145-500-6

The Bully and Me
Stories that Break the Cycle of Violence
by Helen Carmichael Porter
Includes a CD with 3 of the stories from the book
told by the author. The stories in the book are
first person accounts by both victims and bullies
of what happens to real people.
978-1-896836-79-9

Writing the Sacred
A psalm-inspired path to writing sacred poetry
by Ray McGinnis
978-1-896836-73-7

Oil & Water
Two Faiths/One God
by Amir Hussain
An exploration of the Muslim and Christian faiths.
978-1-896836-82-9

How to Be A Perfect Stanger volumes 1 &2:
*Guides to Etiquette in Other People's
Religious Ceremonies*
Stuart M. Matlins and Arthur J. Magida, eds.
978-1-896836-28-7
978-1-89836-29-4

Check your favourite bookstore,
or call 1.800.663.2775 or visit www.woodlakebooks.com